Judaism

Other books in the Introducing Issues with Opposing Viewpoints series:

Abortion
Bullying
Cheating
Child Abuse
Christianity
Death and Dying
The Election Process
Endangered Species
Homosexuality
Illegal Immigration
The Internet
Marijuana
The Middle East
Native Americans
Oil
Prisons
Rap Music
Religion in Schools
Television
The U.S. Government
Water Resource Management
Weapons of Mass Destruction

Judaism

Emma Carlson Berne, *Book Editor*

GREENHAVEN PRESS
A part of Gale, Cengage Learning

Detroit • New York • San Francisco • New Haven, Conn • Waterville, Maine • London

Christine Nasso, *Publisher*
Elizabeth Des Chenes, *Managing Editor*

For more information, contact:
Greenhaven Press
27500 Drake Rd.
Farmington Hills, MI 48331-3535
Or you can visit our Internet site at gale.cengage.com

Articles in Greenhaven Press anthologies are often edited for length to meet page requirements. In addition, original titles of these works are changed to clearly present the main thesis and to explicitly indicate the author's opinion. Every effort is made to ensure that Greenhaven Press accurately reflects the original intent of the authors. Every effort has been made to trace the owners of copyrighted material.

ISBN: 978-0-7377-3976-3

Library of Congress Control Number: 2008923793

Printed in the United States of America
1 2 3 4 5 6 7 12 11 10 09 08

Contents

Chapter 3: What Issues Affect Modern Judaism?

Foreword

Indulging in a wide spectrum of ideas, beliefs, and perspectives is a critical cornerstone of democracy. After all, it is often debates over differences of opinion, such as whether to legalize abortion, how to treat prisoners, or when to enact the death penalty, that shape our society and drive it forward. Such diversity of thought is frequently regarded as the hallmark of a healthy and civilized culture. As the Reverend Clifford Schutjer of the First Congregational Church in Mansfield, Ohio, declared in a 2001 sermon, "Surrounding oneself with only like-minded people, restricting what we listen to or read only to what we find agreeable is irresponsible. Refusing to entertain doubts once we make up our minds is a subtle but deadly form of arrogance." With this advice in mind, Introducing Issues with Opposing Viewpoints books aim to open readers' minds to the critically divergent views that comprise our world's most important debates.

Introducing Issues with Opposing Viewpoints simplifies for students the enormous and often overwhelming mass of material now available via print and electronic media. Collected in every volume is an array of opinions that captures the essence of a particular controversy or topic. Introducing Issues with Opposing Viewpoints books embody the spirit of nineteenth-century journalist Charles A. Dana's axiom: "Fight for your opinions, but do not believe that they contain the whole truth, or the only truth." Absorbing such contrasting opinions teaches students to analyze the strength of an argument and compare it to its opposition. From this process readers can inform and strengthen their own opinions, or be exposed to new information that will change their minds. Introducing Issues with Opposing Viewpoints is a mosaic of different voices. The authors are statesmen, pundits, academics, journalists, corporations, and ordinary people who have felt compelled to share their experiences and ideas in a public forum. Their words have been collected from newspapers, journals, books, speeches, interviews, and the Internet, the fastest growing body of opinionated material in the world.

Introducing Issues with Opposing Viewpoints shares many of the well-known features of its critically acclaimed parent series, Opposing Viewpoints. The articles are presented in a pro/con format, allowing readers to absorb divergent perspectives side by side. Active reading questions preface each viewpoint, requiring the student to approach the material thoughtfully and carefully. Useful charts, graphs, and cartoons supplement each article. A thorough introduction provides readers with crucial background on an issue. An annotated bibliography points the reader toward articles, books, and Web sites that contain additional information on the topic. An appendix of organizations to contact contains a wide variety of charities, nonprofit organizations, political groups, and private enterprises that each hold a position on the issue at hand. Finally, a comprehensive index allows readers to locate content quickly and efficiently.

Introducing Issues with Opposing Viewpoints is also significantly different from Opposing Viewpoints. As the series title implies, its presentation will help introduce students to the concept of opposing viewpoints, and learn to use this material to aid in critical writing and debate. The series' four-color, accessible format makes the books attractive and inviting to readers of all levels. In addition, each viewpoint has been carefully edited to maximize a reader's understanding of the content. Short but thorough viewpoints capture the essence of an argument. A substantial, thought-provoking essay question placed at the end of each viewpoint asks the student to further investigate the issues raised in the viewpoint, compare and contrast two authors' arguments, or consider how one might go about forming an opinion on the topic at hand. Each viewpoint contains sidebars that include at-a-glance information and handy statistics. A Facts About section located in the back of the book further supplies students with relevant facts and figures.

Following in the tradition of the Opposing Viewpoints series, Greenhaven Press continues to provide readers with invaluable exposure to the controversial issues that shape our world. As John Stuart Mill once wrote: "The only way in which a human being can make some approach to knowing the whole of a subject is by hearing what can be said about it by persons of every variety of opinion and studying all modes in which it can be looked at by every character of mind. No wise man ever acquired his wisdom in any mode but this." It is to this principle that Introducing Issues with Opposing Viewpoints books are dedicated.

Introduction

"It has been a hallmark of my maturity to lay claim to Americanness and Judaism. The problem is to locate an identity that is authentic, without assuming positions I do not fit."

—Andrew Solomon, *New Statesman*, 2004

Out of the 6.5 billion people on the planet, only 14 million are Jews—only 0.2 percent of the global population. In the United States, which holds 40 percent of the total world Jewish population, only 1.78 percent of the population is Jewish, according to the Jewish Virtual Library. Judaism is a tiny religion, yet the issues that affect the Jewish people often have far-reaching consequences.

Traditionally, Jewish people have long been nomads, traveling from country to country over the centuries in search of a society that would accept them. Often, Jews were persecuted, killed, or driven from their chosen homelands. The Jews were expelled from Spain during the time of Columbus: As the famous explorer's ship pulled out of the dock at Palos, Spain, on August 3, 1492, the shores were thronged with Jews ordered to either get out of Spain or convert to Christianity. Jews in rural villages were attacked and killed and their property burned during pogroms—riots—against them in nineteenth-century Russia. The Nazis of World War II Germany managed to kill almost 66 percent of all the Jews in Europe.

Centuries of persecution have deeply affected modern global Jewry. Many feel that the Jewish people must stick together, protect themselves, and find safe refuge so that the crimes of the past can never be repeated. Indeed, holding together as a distinct group has been a defining characteristic of modern Judaism since its beginnings.

Jews are sometimes referred to, by themselves or others, as "the chosen people," a phrase which stems from God's reference to the Israelites in the biblical book of Exodus. Many of the controversial issues surrounding Judaism today reflect the belief that the Jewish people should maintain a degree of separation from the non-Jewish world. Jews should live within a society, some say, but keep cultural boundaries distinct.

Judaism is a religion centered around the practice of daily, weekly, monthly, and yearly ritual. The laws governing these rituals are laid out in a book called the Talmud, a vast text of both biblical religious law and extensive commentaries on that law. The Talmud includes laws that govern the keeping of the Sabbath and those that instruct rituals for birth, circumcision, coming of age, marriage, and death. There are dietary laws, laws for prayer, daily life, relationships between all sorts of different people, political action, moral behavior, and even laws for washing and hygiene.

The purpose of all of these rituals is to bring the practitioner closer to God. But often, Jewish observance and practice also serve to divide Jews from others in society and affirm the place of Jews as a people separate and distinct. The most extreme example is that of ultra-Orthodox Jews, who live in communities closed to outsiders and try to limit their interaction with the non-Jewish world.

In the United States, most Jews are assimilated into American society and thus occasionally struggle with the very rituals that help define their religious and cultural identity. A traditional Jewish circumcision, for instance, takes place in the family home, with a mohel, a circumciser, performing the ritual. Some Jewish parents, though, opt to have a physician circumcise their sons in a hospital. Others have chosen to give up circumcising entirely. A 2007 article in the *Toronto Star* reports that American circumcision levels have fallen from a peak of 84 percent to 57 percent in recent years—including a decrease in religious circumcision by Jews. One Jewish mother is quoted in a 2007 *Toronto Star* article as saying, "I see circumcision as a blood ritual that I can let go of."

Today, most Jews have found their place in the world—whether in the United States, Israel, Europe, or elsewhere. But cultural boundaries the Jewish people have maintained over the centuries have also contributed to prejudice and persecution in both the past and the present. Some are suspicious of a people who want to live within a society but not integrate into it—who want to marry among each other and follow their own customs, even through generations.

Anti-Semitism is a major concern in modern Judaism. Amiram Barkat reported in the Israeli newspaper *Haaretz* in July 2007 that hate crimes against Jews had risen in Europe, so far that year, as much as 6 percent in countries such as Germany. Many believe that ignoring anti-Semitic attacks could open the door to wide-scale persecution such as Jews have experienced in the past. "It doesn't take long for hatred toward one group of people to redirect itself as hatred toward Jews," write Marnina Cherkin and Amy M. Stein, assistant directors of the Jewish advocacy group the Anti-Defamation League. "History has shown us that wherever hate breeds, it is bad for the Jews. Whenever it has been acceptable to discriminate against any people, it has been bad for the Jews."

The creation of the state of Israel as a Jewish homeland helped combat some of the fears left by the worst persecution of Jews—the Holocaust. Yet the desire to shield, insulate, and protect from the outside world and its dangers still manifests itself when Jews are scolded for not wholeheartedly supporting the Israeli people and the policies of their government. The argument over Zionism and "anti-Zionism" is another key controversy affecting the Jewish people. When some Jews don't "follow the rules" and support Israel, some fear the entire Jewish people are put at risk for genocide. Other Jews, however, believe that disagreement with the policies of the Israeli government should not be considered a betrayal of the Jewish people.

The controversies affecting Judaism are complex and nuanced. Many stem from struggles between tradition and modernity, between protection of the Jewish culture and assimilation into society. *Introducing Issues with Opposing Viewpoints: Judaism* clarifies and illuminates the key issues affecting Jews and Judaism today.

Chapter 1

Is Anti-Semitism a Serious Problem for Modern Jews?

Anti-Semitic graffiti is one sign people point to of growing negativity toward Jews in Europe.

Anti-Semitism Is Still a Serious Problem

Tish Durkin

"It will come as no surprise to tolerant Arabs that anti-Semitism runs wide and deep in their political culture."

Tish Durkin is a journalist who writes for the *New York Times* and *Atlantic Monthly* as well as *National Journal.* In the following viewpoint Durkin argues that anti-Semitism, prejudice against Jews is widespread in the Arab world. Durkin writes that she encountered many anti-Semitic comments and beliefs during her work in the Middle East. Anti-Semitism is not universal among Arabs, Durkin writes, but the prejudice is strong where it exists. Overcoming it will require a concerted and sustained effort, she states.

AS YOU READ, CONSIDER THE FOLLOWING QUESTIONS:

1. What are the two news items named by the author that have caused her to think about anti-Semitism?
2. What is one reason given by the author as to why many Arabs are ready to believe absurd theories of current events?
3. What gesture did some non-Muslim American women make to emphasize that they do not equate terrorism with Islam?

Tish Durkin, "You Know, David Letterman Doesn't Run America," *National Journal,* vol. 34, March 2, 2002, pp. 588–589.

Encountering anti-Semitism in the Arab world is like seeing the Grand Canyon for the first time: You think that you are prepared for the immensity of it and the endless variations of expression within it. But until you are standing there, believing and disbelieving it, you just have no idea.

Anti-Semitism comes to mind because of two . . . items in the news [in 2002]. One is the nine-nation Gallup Poll showing that most Muslims do not believe that Arabs perpetrated the acts of September 11; the other is the news of the short life and sudden death of the Office of Strategic Influence, which was described in *The New York Times* as a "small but well-financed" Defense Department operation that had been formed to sweeten foreign coverage of the war on terrorism, and that had a brief but tortured liaison with veracity [truth]. First, Pentagon officials privately reserved the right to lie in the line of duty. Then, they officially promised not to lie, but refused to promise that their public relations contractors would not lie. Finally, they declared that nobody would lie.

Deep Divide Between American and Arab Worlds

The poll underscores the huge perceptual gap that exists between America and the Arab world, a gap that would exist, to the detriment of both sides, even if there were no war on terrorism. The Office of Strategic Influence interlude scarily illustrates how needlessly wrongheaded America has been in closing that gap. Anti-Semitism is one of the several major factors that comprise the gap—and that would have been left wholly untouched by the Pentagon's semisecret machinations.

FAST FACT

While the term "anti-Semitism" is widely used to describe anti-Jewish prejudice, it is technically inaccurate. A Semite is any one of a number of ethnic groups from southeastern Asia, including Arabs.

Let me be clear: I don't mean to brand all Arabs with a characteristic that is, of course, present in our own culture, nor to equate all anti-Israel sentiment with anti-Semitism. (Obviously, the two frequently overlap, but not always.) That said, it

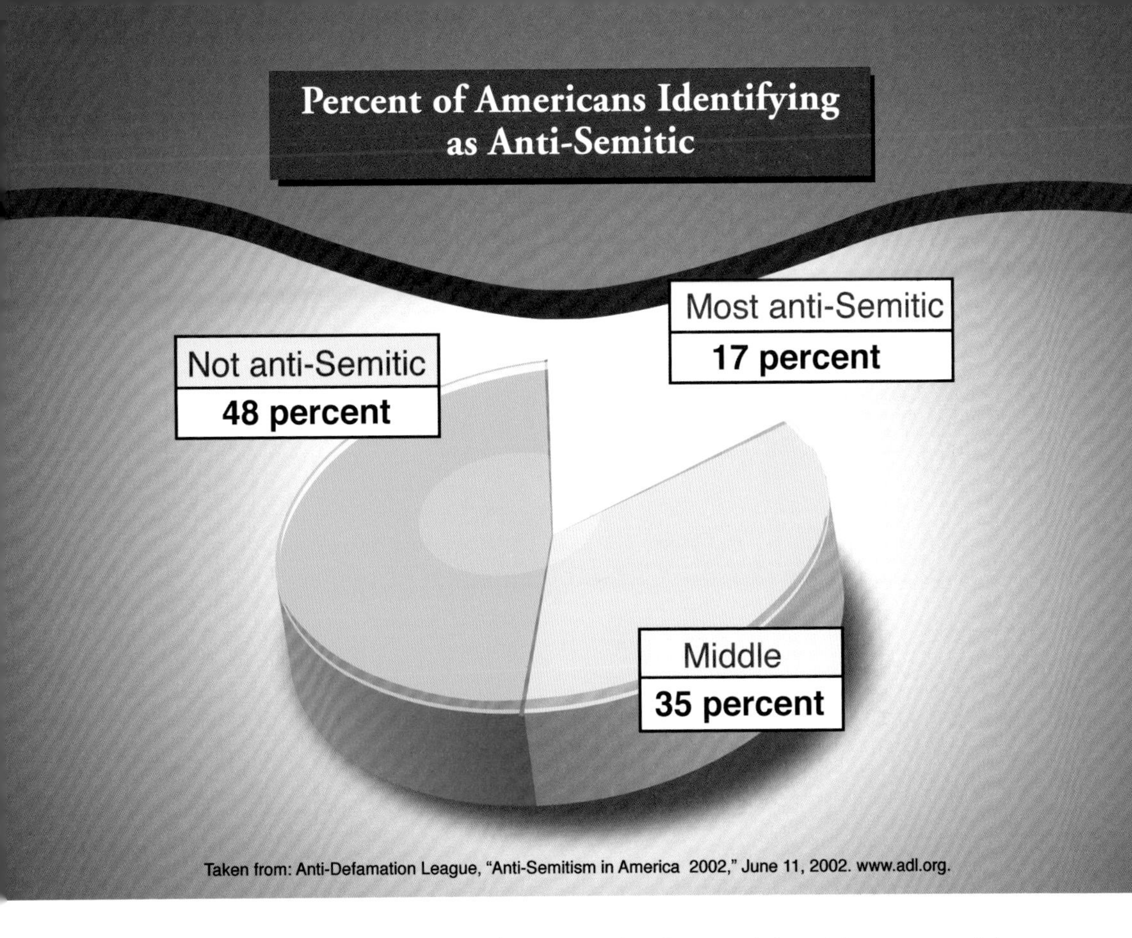

will come as no surprise to tolerant Arabs that anti-Semitism runs wide and deep in their political culture, and it is no compliment to them to pretend otherwise. In fact, the way that one acquires confidence that anti-Semitism is not a universal here is that, where it is present, it walks right up and introduces itself.

Examples of Anti-Semitism

Sometimes it introduces itself chillingly, as it did when Tareq Al-Kandery, the 23-year-old chairman of the National Union of Kuwait Students, informed me that he did not consider organizations such as Islamic Jihad and Hamas to be terrorist in nature, and that he deemed their causes so just as to allow for "even the killing of a Muslim . . . if the killing of that Muslim will help with the killing of more Israelis."

Sometimes it introduces itself on a note of unintentional humor, as it did one day in Kuwait. After a couple of interviews in a row in which "the Jewish lobby" had come up with a little too much frequency and contempt for comfort, I vented a little to my government press liaison, a sunny young man who had spent several years being educated in the United States. I was not taking notes, so the following quotes are not exact, but the gist is factual.

"Why? Why do people think that the United States is run by a cabal [a group of secret plotters] of Jews? We've never had a Jewish President."

"I know, but people look at that guy who worked for [Bill] Clinton and think he's really running things."

"Who?"

"The bald guy, little eyes."

"James Carville [former Clinton Campaign Manager]?"

"Yeah!"

"James Carville isn't Jewish!"

"Yes he is."

"No he isn't! He's Catholic . . . I think."

"OK: David Letterman."

I have had dozens of these conversations. An alternative version is to be given the name of a prominent American who actually is Jewish, and then to find yourself explaining how, in the overall scheme of things, that person does not really possess a disproportionate, mysterious power. It is that easy to slip on the ice of the assumption that the presence of individuals who really are Jewish in positions that really are significant constitutes a demerit of some kind.

Anti-Semitism Is Everywhere

Anti-Semitism can walk right up and knock you in the head out of nowhere, as when you are at a lovely party, talking about the weather and the food and the pretty dress you have on, and it comes up that the Holocaust never happened, or that it has been blown way, way out of proportion. I have not personally had any conversations with anyone who has asserted that the attacks of September 11 were perpetrated by Jews in an effort to smear Muslims, but I have had many conversations with people who have described that mentality in their own community.

Moreover, what is true for all these anti-Semitic myths is true for other anti-American myths that live in the Arab world: They are wildly wrong, easily punctured by fact, and maddeningly resilient anyway.

They are also supremely ironic. In so many conversations, I feel as if the person speaking to me has whipped out a blindingly reflective cultural mirror and turned it on the West. So many people here see so many post-September 11 American actions—not just the bombing of Afghanistan, but also basic tightening-ups in the areas of security and immigration—as acts of discrimination against Muslims, that I can't help but attribute it in part to the fact that their own societies so frankly institutionalize discrimination against non-Muslims.

An Italian police officer looks down on a Jewish cemetery marker that has been knocked over and broken.

Hard Work to Overcome Prejudice

One reason why many Arabs are so ready to pull the most absurd theory of current events out of thin air is that they have never had any good reason to believe the account of current events given by their government-controlled media. It is far too long and winding a road to reach any full conclusion about any of this. But for strategic-influence purposes, suffice it to say: Given the challenges that are huge and utterly negative (anti-Semitism), and the challenges that are huge and utterly complicated (love-hate relationship with pluralism), the most wonderfully assembled and outfitted American propaganda effort would be a climb up the slippery side of Everest.

This does not mean that the climb is not worth attempting. Make no mistake: People here did notice that the President [George W. Bush] visited the Islamic Center in Washington after September 11, and that he invited Muslim leaders to the White House to break the Ramadan fast. Some of them even noticed, and deeply appreciated, the gesture made by the non-Muslim American women who covered their heads to emphasize that they did not equate terrorism with Islam. It's not that such efforts don't work. It's that they don't work miracles. To keep working, they have to keep happening—and they have to keep happening at a more engaged and messier level than the best photo ops can allow for.

EVALUATING THE AUTHOR'S ARGUMENTS:

In the viewpoint you just read, author Tish Durkin offers several personal examples of anti-Semitic incidents she encountered while traveling in the Middle East. Durkin describes these incidents in a casual, humorous way. Do you think these examples add to or detract from her argument? Explain your answer.

The Problem of Anti-Semitism Has Been Exaggerated

"If both sides agree on anything, it's that the definition of 'anti-Semitism' has been manipulated for political ends."

Michael Neumann

In the following viewpoint author Michael Neumann argues that anti-Semitism has been made to seem a larger problem than it actually is. Part of this results from how anti-Semitism is defined, Neumann writes. Certain groups consider any person, even if Jewish, anti-Semitic if they criticize Israel or its actions. Under this definition, almost anyone could be anti-Semitic. Moreover, Neumann states, there are many other groups who have experienced murder and death in far greater numbers than Jews. Michael Neumann is a professor of philosophy at Trent University in Canada.

AS YOU READ, CONSIDER THE FOLLOWING QUESTIONS:

1. According to the author, of what do leftists accuse Zionists in the debate over anti-Semitism?
2. Using context from the article, define "canards."
3. What is the best way to define anti-Semitism, according to the viewpoint?

Michael Neumann, "A Minor Problem, Overblown," *www.miftah.org,* December 28, 2003. Reproduced by permission.

Jewish and non-Jewish commentators alike have deplored [an] upsurge in anti-Semitism. In Europe, journalist Andrew Sullivan says, "Not since the 1930s has such blithe hatred of Jews gained this much respectability in world opinion."

Yet, Jews like myself and the Israeli journalist Ran HaCohen feel quite differently. He writes: "It is high time to say it out loud: In the entire course of Jewish history, since the Babylonian exile in the 6th century B.C. there has never been an era blessed with less anti-Semitism than ours. There has never been a better time for Jews to live in than our own."

Struggles to Define Anti-Semitism

Why would a Jew say such a thing? What is anti-Semitism, and how much of a danger is it in the world today? If both sides agree on anything, it's that the definition of "anti-Semitism" has been manipulated for political ends. Leftists accuse ardent Zionists of inflating the definition to include—and discredit—critics of Israel. Zionists accuse the left of deflating the definition to apologize for covert prejudice against Jews.

It's a sterile dispute. Even in this age of intellectual property, no one owns the word. But the definitional sparring does have its missteps and dangers.

The first tells against deflationists who claim that anti-Semitism is really hatred of Semites (including Arabs), not just Jews. [Semites are defined as any of a group of people from the Near East and North Africa, including Arabs, Jews, and Ethiopians.] This confuses etymology with meaning. You might as well say that, in reality, lesbians are simply those who live on the Greek island of Lesbos. [The term "lesbian" derives from the poems of the ancient Greek poet Sappho, born on the isle of Lesbos.]

On the other hand, to inflate the definition by including critics of Israel is, if not exactly incorrect, self-defeating and dangerous. No one can stop you from proclaiming all criticism of Israel anti-Semitic. But

Fast Fact

The term "anti-Semitism" was first used in 1879 by German agitator Wilhelm Marr when he founded "The League of Antisemites," an organization dedicated to removing the Jewish presence from Germany.

While anti-Semitism may be declining in the United States, acts of vandalism and violence against Jews have risen in Europe.

that makes anti-Semites out of [former South African president] Nelson Mandela and Bishop Desmond Tutu [a peace activist] not to mention tens of thousands of Jews.

Responsibility to Do Good Is Not Anti-Semitism

What then prevents someone from concluding that anti-Semitism must be, at least in some cases, justifiable, courageous, highly moral? Is this a message any prudent Jew or anti-racist would want to encourage?

Similar worries arise when Abraham H. Foxman, national director of the Anti-Defamation League, tells us: "The classic canards of 'Jews control,' 'Jews are responsible' and 'Jews are not loyal' continue to be peddled in America. While anti-Semites have usually been on the fringes of our society, today we find they and their views have made it into the mainstream."

Well, it might be anti-Semitic to hold Jews responsible for everything, but it would be bizarre to claim anti-Semitism whenever Jews are held responsible for anything. In a [2002] survey conducted by Steven M. Cohen of the Hebrew University of Jerusalem, 87% of American Jews said that Jews "have a responsibility to work on behalf of the poor, the oppressed and minority groups"; 92% said that Jews are obliged to help other Jews who are "needy or oppressed." What Foxman calls an anti-Semitic canard is deeply rooted in traditional and contemporary Jewish thought. A Web search will find dozens of rabbis attributing to Jews, generally, not just responsibilities but collective responsibility.

We hold groups responsible for things, good and bad, all the time: The Germans started World War II, the French opposed us in Iraq, the British supported us. The strongly pro-Israel columnist Jonathan Rosenblum states, "The Jews have built an advanced, industrial state, while the Palestinians have built nothing."

Clearly, it is not just anti-Semites who attribute responsibility to the Jews. And just as clearly, this is neither racist nor to be taken literally. Rosenblum does not mean that every last Jew, including children and the mentally disabled, built that state. He means that most adult Jews made some contribution to it.

Criticism of Israel Is Not Anti-Semitic

If so, should definitional inflation be allowed to make anti-Semites out of all those who hold Jews responsible for Israel's actions and character? My childhood, in largely Jewish suburbs of New York and Boston, was full of Israel bond drives and calls to support Israel. Can't Rosenblum say that "the Jews," meaning a substantial majority of adult Jews, have some responsibility for what Israel has become? And can't Amnesty International or Human Rights Watch say that Israel has committed war crimes and violated human rights?

One might justly call it dangerous to conclude that Jews, generally, had some responsibility for war crimes and human rights violations. But to call it anti-Semitic seems just as dangerous, because in some loose, though not unreasonable, sense, the conclusion is hard to escape. That's why there are whole Jewish organizations, like

Not in My Name, that exist to enable Jews to dissociate themselves from Israel's actions.

Anti-Semitism Is Hatred of Jews

In short, you can't have it both ways. You can, if you like, inflate the definition of "anti-Semitism" to capture even Jewish political opponents of Israel. But you can't do this and keep "anti-Semitism" as a term of intense moral condemnation. Nor will the inflationary gambit successfully isolate the truly reprehensible anti-Semites.

The best way to reserve "anti-Semitism" as a term of condemnation is to define it as hatred of Jews, not for what they do but for what they are. It is to hate them just because they belong to a certain ethnic group. Foxman is right to suggest that you can be an anti-Semite

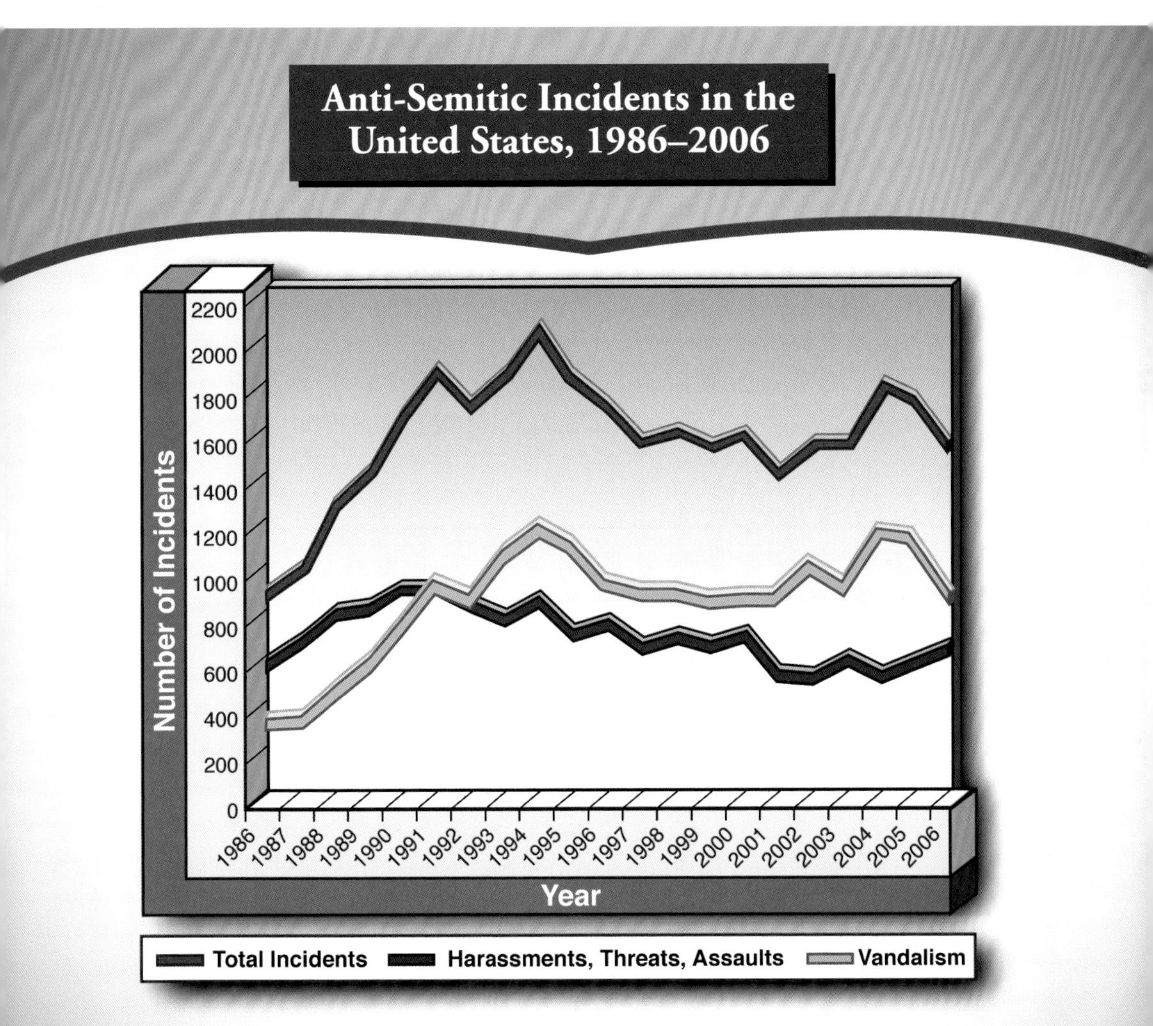

Taken from: Anti-Defamation League, "Anti-Semitic Incidents in U.S. Decline in 2006, Despite Year Marked by Violent Attacks," March 14, 2007. www.adl.org.

without expressing any racist sentiments. Many anti-Semites confine themselves to expounding false claims about Jewish control. But you can also, without harboring anti-Semitic hate, criticize Israel and even the Jewish community for its failures. To suppose otherwise would be to suppose an inexplicable wave of anti-Semitism among both American and Israeli Jews, both of whom figure prominently among the critics.

But the touchiest question is not what anti-Semitism is, or whether it has increased. It is whether Jews are in significant danger. Isn't that what matters? To put it personally: Anti-Semitism may be important to me, but is it important, period? The answer cannot be dictated by "Jewish sensibilities."

My background certainly predisposes me to regard anti-Semitic incidents with alarm. But time passes. Concentration camp survivors still alive deserve sympathy and justice, but they are few. Myself, I'd feel a bit embarrassed saying to a homeless person on the streets of Toronto, much less to the inhabitants of a Philippine garbage dump: "Oh yeah? You think you know suffering? My grandmother died in a concentration camp!"

Anti-Semitism Is Minor Compared to Other Problems

We should indeed guard against a resurgence of European fascism, and Jewish organizations are oddly lax about this. The ADL [Anti-Defamation League], for instance, did not comment on last month's [November 2003] electoral gains of Croatian nationalists who trace their lineage directly back to some of Adolf Hitler's most savage and willing executioners. But we Jews live not in the past but in a brutal present that forces us to reassess our moral priorities.

An appropriately stark reassessment might involve counting up the dead and wounded in the ADL's list of anti-Semitic incidents in 2002 and 2003. Its surveys include two Al Qaeda attacks. This is questionable: Al Qaeda's war on the United States, Israel, the West and pretty much everyone else seems independent of sentiment in the countries in which the attacks occurred. Include these attacks and the number of Jews killed in that period seems to be nine. Exclude them, and it falls to one, in Morocco. Jews hospitalized or incurring serious injuries falls to about a dozen.

On March 14 [2002], the BBC reported that the Honduran government would investigate the killings of 1,569 street children in the last five years. The killers may well be "police or army personnel," according to Amnesty International, and there have been virtually no prosecutions. Not even the alternative left-wing press gave the story any coverage. In the Congo, 3 million have died in 4 1/2 years. Perhaps anti-Semitism is not, after all, a high priority.

EVALUATING THE AUTHOR'S ARGUMENTS:

Author Michael Neumann provides several definitions of anti-Semitism in this viewpoint. One is "inflated," one is "deflated," and one is just right, in his opinion. Identify each definition in the viewpoint and review it. Then decide which one you agree with and state why.

Viewpoint 3

Anti-Zionism Is Anti-Semitism

Abraham H. Foxman

"Anti-Zionism is anti-Semitism. There should be no debate about that. After all, what is anti-Zionism but the denial of Jewish nationalism?"

Abraham H. Foxman is the director of the Anti-Defamation League, a Jewish advocacy group. In the following viewpoint Foxman argues that while criticism of Israel can be legitimate, anti-Zionism is equal to anti-Semitism. To be against Zionism is to be against Jewish nationalism, Foxman writes, and thus, against the Jewish people and their continued existence. It is perfectly acceptable to criticize specific Israeli policies but not the entire Jewish state and its people.

AS YOU READ, CONSIDER THE FOLLOWING QUESTIONS:

1. Foxman states that the Jewish people have developed "litmus tests" to find out if criticism of Israel is over the line. Name one of these test questions.
2. According to the author, what did the UN "Zionism is racism" resolution say, in essence?
3. Define the phrase "blurring the line" as it is used in the author's argument.

Invariably, the most frequent question I am asked is, "Can't I be critical of Israel or be anti-Zionist without being labeled an anti-Semite?" Invariably, my answer is, "Yes, but . . ." And it is with that "but" that I try to make the questioner understand how easily the line can be crossed between legitimate criticism of a sovereign nation, and the demonization and delegitimization of the Jewish people, its nationalism and its state.

I tell the questioner that everyone has the right to criticize Israel, just as they have the right to criticize the United States, Great Britain, Argentina, Taiwan or Nigeria. Even harsh condemnation of Israeli policy is not on its own anti-Semitic, and it is irresponsible to brand every critic of Israel as an enemy of the Jewish people. Indeed, I say, some of the toughest criticism of Israel is to be found in the Israeli press, which is as free and multivoiced as any in the world.

Anti-Zionism Is Code for Anti-Semitism

However, we have developed a number of litmus tests to assess when criticism of Israel crosses the line. Is Israel being repeatedly singled out for criticism and blame? Is Israel being held to a double standard—being denounced while a blind eye is turned to the excesses and offenses of other nations? Is it Israeli policy that is the subject of criticism, or is it the existence of the Jewish state and Jews as a whole?

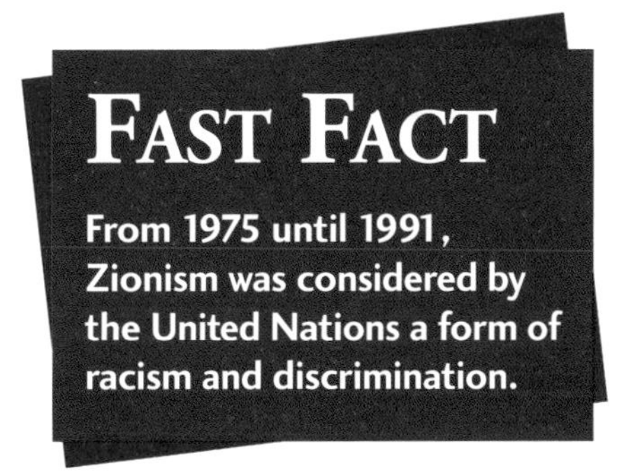

The Palestinian-Israeli conflict has been hijacked, resulting in an explosion of global anti-Semitism. It has provided a camouflage of semi-respectability. The attacks are not about a nation state, they are about Jews. A hideous and grotesque double standard clearly exists in my mind. Anti-Zionism has long been a code word for anti-Semitism. We have had to define for ourselves when anti-Israel and anti-Zionism is anti-Semitism.

First, let me say anti-Zionism is anti-Semitism. There should be no debate about that. After all, what is anti-Zionism but the denial

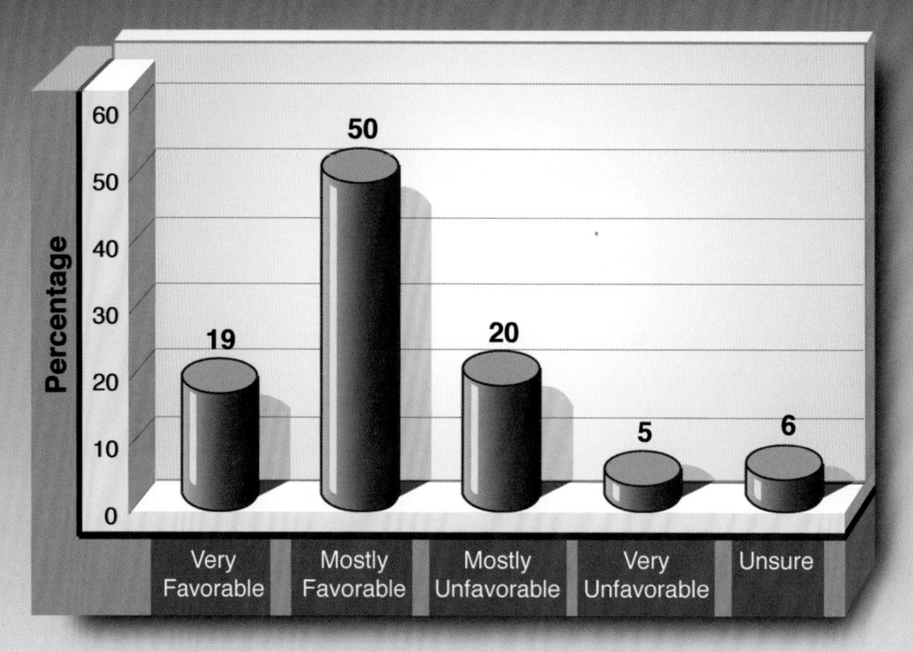

Taken from: Gallup poll, "Israel and the Palestinians," February 7–10, 2005.

of Jewish nationalism? Nothing made it clearer than when it came out in the UN's [1975] "Zionism racism" resolution. It is pure, simple, unadulterated anti-Semitism. What it says is what is okay, what is permissible, what is laudatory, what is universally accepted for all peoples in the world—self-expression, self-determination, independence, sovereignty—is not permitted to Jews. That is what it says. It doesn't say Irish nationalism is racist or Congolese nationalism or French or Palestinian nationalism. It says Jewish nationalism is racist. That is pure and simple anti-Semitism. . . .

Legitimate Criticism vs. Anti-Semitism

There are also the questions: Is the newspaper article or editorial anti-Israel or anti-Semitic? Is the columnist anti-Israel or anti-Semitic? We have developed guidelines here, too. . . . Those who only find fault with the Jewish people, the Jewish state and the actions of the Jewish sovereignty, and never find anything that is positive, are anti-Semites under the guise of anti-Zionism and anti-Israel sentiment.

The fact is that the cumulative effect of articles by so-called anti-Israel critics leads to a blurring of the line of what is legitimate criticism of policies of the State of Israel, and what is the demonization of Jews. The result is the raising of society's tolerance level for anti-Semitism.

In the most extreme examples, this tolerance for anti-Semitism has resulted in the justification of egregious acts of anti-Semitism as merely an expression of opposition to Israeli policies. When anti-Jewish violence erupted across France, government leaders, the media and other opinion-molders were hesitant to denounce it as anti-Semitism, because the torching of synagogues in their minds was understood within the context of the Arab-Israeli conflict. Today, the international community sits in virtual silence when media in the Arab/Muslim world promote through their propaganda the most heinous conspiracy theories about Jews, because it is viewed through the prism of criticism of Israel.

Anti-Zionist rabbis meet with Iranian president Mahmoud Ahmadinejad, far left, who is considered an enemy of Israel.

Opponents of specific Israeli policies can argue their position based on facts and opinions, and they can expect to be challenged by supporters of these Israeli policies on the merits of such arguments. However, when that criticism is directed at the entire Jewish people or questions the legitimacy of the Jewish state, it is an expression of anti-Semitism.

EVALUATING THE AUTHOR'S ARGUMENTS:

Abraham H. Foxman, the author of this viewpoint, believes that criticizing the *existence* of the state of Israel is the same as being anti-Semitic. Do you agree or disagree with this argument? Is it possible for someone not to believe that Israel should exist, yet still be accepting of Jewish people?

Anti-Zionism Is Not Anti-Semitism

"You do not have to be an anti-semite to reject the belief that Jews constitute a separate nation . . . or that Israel is the Jewish nation state."

Brian Klug

In the following viewpoint author Brian Klug argues that it is indeed possible for someone to hold anti-Zionist beliefs and yet not be an anti-Semite. In fact, Klug points out, many Jews were against Zionism when the idea was first developed during the nineteenth century. Moreover, he writes, Israel is a political nation. Judaism is a religion and a culture. It is possible to separate the two, Klug argues, fully supporting Jews and yet not supporting Israel or its policies. Brian Klug is a research fellow in philosophy at Oxford University.

AS YOU READ, CONSIDER THE FOLLOWING QUESTIONS:

1. Using context from the article, define the term "post-Zionism."
2. How does the author specifically describe an anti-Semite?
3. Locate the quote in the viewpoint from Alan Dershowitz and explain its meaning.

Brian Klug, "No, Anti-Zionism Is Not Anti-Semitism," *The Guardian* (London), December 3, 2003.

From the beginning, political Zionism was a controversial movement even among Jews. So strong was the opposition of German orthodox and reform rabbis to the Zionist idea in the name of Judaism that [founder of modern Zionism] Theodor Herzl changed the venue of the First Zionist Congress in 1897 from Munich to Basle in Switzerland.

Twenty years later, when the British foreign secretary, Arthur Balfour (sponsor of the 1905 Aliens Act to restrict Jewish immigration to the UK), wanted the government to commit itself to a Jewish homeland in Palestine, his declaration was delayed—not by anti-semites but by leading figures in the British Jewish community. They included a Jewish member of the cabinet who called Balfour's pro-Zionism "anti-semitic in result".

FAST FACT

Journalist Leonard Fein of *Forward* reports that in a recent survey of Jews, only 28 percent considered themselves Zionists.

Israel's National Identity

The creation of the state of Israel in 1948 has not put an end to the debate, though the issue has changed. Today, the question is about Israel's future. Should it become a "post-Zionist" state, one that defines itself in terms of the sum of its citizens, rather than seeing itself as belonging to the entire Jewish people? This is a perfectly legitimate question and not anti-semitic in the least. When people suggest otherwise . . . they simply add to the growing confusion.

[Oxford University professor Emanuele] Ottolenghi contends that "Zionism comprises a belief that Jews are a nation, and as such are entitled to self-determination as all other nations are". This is doubly confused. First, the ideology of Jewish nationalism was irrelevant to many of the Jews, as well as non-Jewish sympathisers, who were drawn to the Zionist goal of creating a Jewish state in Palestine. They saw Israel in purely humanitarian or practical terms: as a safe haven where Jews could live as Jews after centuries of being marginalised and persecuted.

This motive was strengthened by the Nazi murder of one-third of the world's Jewish population, the wholesale destruction of Jewish communities in Europe, and the plight of masses of Jewish refugees with nowhere to go.

A Definition of Anti-Semitism

Second, you do not have to be an anti-semite to reject the belief that Jews constitute a separate nation in the modern sense of the word or that Israel is the Jewish nation state. There is an irony here: it is a staple of anti-semitic discourse that Jews are a people apart, who form "a state within a state". Partly for this reason, some European anti-semites

Some anti-Zionists believe that the existence of Israel, as a Jewish state, has led to increased anti-Semitism.

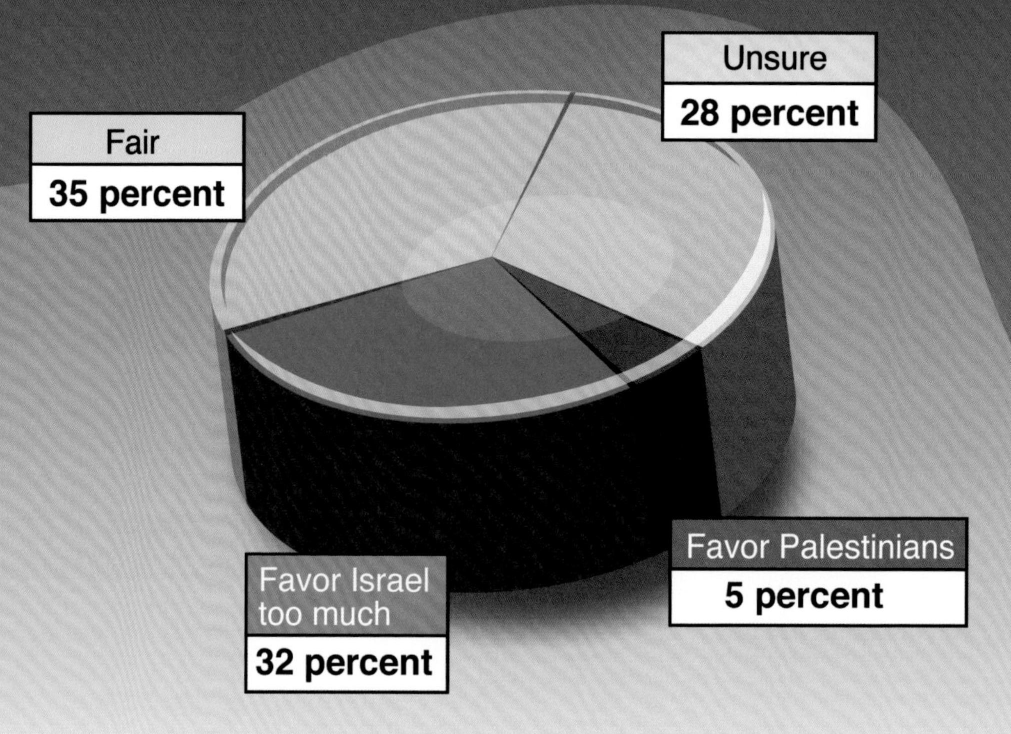

Taken from: Pew Research Center/Council on Foreign Relations, "Foreign Policy Attitudes Now Driven by 9/11 and Iraq," August 18, 2004.

thought that the solution to "the Jewish question" might be for Jews to have a state of their own. Herzl certainly thought he could count on the support of anti-semites.

What is anti-semitism? Although the word only goes back to the 1870s, anti-semitism is an old European fantasy about Jews. The composer Richard Wagner exemplified it when he said: "I hold the Jewish race to be the born enemy of pure humanity and everything noble in it." An anti-semite sees Jews this way: they are an alien presence, a parasite that preys on humanity and seeks to dominate the world. Across the globe, their hidden hand controls the banks, the markets and the media. Even governments are under their sway. And when revolutions occur or nations go to war, it is the Jews—clever, ruthless and cohesive—who invariably pull the strings and reap the rewards.

Opposition to Israel Is Acceptable

When this fantasy is projected on to Israel because it is a Jewish state, then anti-Zionism is anti-semitic. And when zealous critics of Israel, without themselves being anti-semitic, carelessly use language, such as "Jewish influence", that conjures up this fantasy, they are fuelling an anti-semitic current in the wider culture.

But Israel's occupation of the West Bank and Gaza Strip is no fantasy. Nor is the spread of Jewish settlements in these territories. Nor the unequal treatment of Jewish colonizers and Palestinian inhabitants. Nor the institutionalized discrimination against Israeli Arab citizens in various spheres of life. These are realities. It is one thing to oppose Israel or Zionism on the basis of an anti-semitic fantasy; quite another to do so on the basis of reality. The latter is not anti-semitism.

But isn't excessive criticism of Israel or Zionism evidence of an anti-semitic bias? In his book, *The Case for Israel*, [Harvard law professor] Alan Dershowitz argues that when criticism of Israel "crosses the line from fair to foul" it goes "from acceptable to anti-semitic".

People who take this view say the line is crossed when critics single Israel out unfairly; when they apply a double standard and judge Israel by harsher criteria than they use for other states; when they misrepresent the facts so as to put Israel in a bad light; when they vilify the Jewish state; and so on. All of which undoubtedly is foul. But is it necessarily anti-semitic?

Reject All Racist Attitudes

No, it is not. The Israeli-Palestinian conflict is a bitter political struggle. The issues are complex, passions are inflamed, and the suffering is great. In such circumstances, people on both sides are liable to be partisan and to "cross the line from fair to foul". When people who side with Israel cross that line, they are not necessarily anti-Muslim. And when others cross the line on behalf of the Palestinian cause, this does not make them anti-Jewish. It cuts both ways.

There is something else that cuts both ways: racism. Both anti-Jewish and anti-Muslim feeling appear to be growing. Each has its own peculiarities, but both are exacerbated by the Israeli-Palestinian conflict, the invasion of Iraq, the "war against terror", and other conflicts.

We should unite in rejecting racism in all its forms: the Islamophobia that demonises Muslims, as well as the anti-semitic discourse that can infect anti-Zionism and poison the political debate. However, people of goodwill can disagree politically—even to the extent of arguing over Israel's future as a Jewish state. Equating anti-Zionism with anti-semitism can also, in its own way, poison the political debate.

EVALUATING THE AUTHORS' ARGUMENTS:

In the viewpoint you just read, author Brian Klug states that it is entirely possible to oppose the state of Israel and yet not hold anti-Semitic beliefs. The author of the previous viewpoint, Abraham H. Foxman, disagrees. He believes it is the duty of Jews to support Israel's existence, even if they oppose certain policies. Not to do so is to be anti-Jewish, or anti-Semitic. With which argument do you agree? Support your answer with evidence from the viewpoints.

Anti-Semitism and Anti-Muslim Prejudice Are Comparable

"Despite important differences, the treatment of British Jews provides an illuminating comparison with contemporary anti-Muslim racism."

Maleiha Malik

Maleiha Malik is a law lecturer at King's College London. In the following viewpoint she argues that modern treatment of Muslims in Britain is very similar to the treatment of Jewish immigrants holding Communist beliefs in the early twentieth century. In both cases, Malik writes, the media and the government treated the immigrants as aliens. People saw the groups as racial outsiders who did not have the characteristics of a British citizen. We must avoid repeating the past, Malik urges, and resist the temptation to vilify certain ethnic and religious groups.

AS YOU READ, CONSIDER THE FOLLOWING QUESTIONS:

1. What are three defining behaviors or customs of the Jewish immigrants?
2. Define the term "folk devil."
3. What is the recurring pattern in recent British history that Malik identifies?

Maleiha Malik, "Muslims Are Now Getting the Same Treatment Jews Had a Century Ago," *The Guardian* (London), February 2, 2007, p. 35.

Migrants fleeing persecution and poverty settled with their children in the East End of London. As believers in one God they were devoted to their holy book, which contained strict religious laws, harsh penalties and gender inequality. Some of them established separate religious courts. The men wore dark clothes and had long beards; some women covered their hair. A royal commission warned of the grave dangers of self-segregation. Politicians said different religious dress was a sign of separation. Some migrants were members of extremist political groups. Others actively organised to overthrow the established western political order. Campaigners against the migrants carefully framed their arguments as objections to "alien extremists" and not to a race or religion. A British cabinet minister said we were facing a clash about civilisation: this was about values; a battle between progress and "arrested development".

Opinions on Muslim Immigration to the United States

This chart shows the poll results for a question gauging Americans' opinions on the number of Muslim immigrants allowed into the United States.

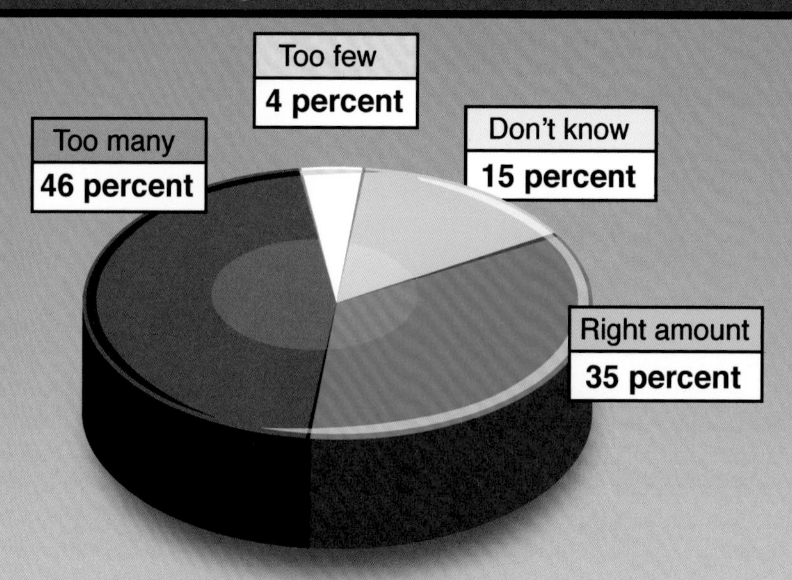

Taken from: *Newsweek*, "Americans Are Mixed on U.S. Muslims," July 20, 2007. www.msnbcmsn.com.

All this happened a hundred years ago to Jewish migrants seeking asylum in Britain. The political movements with which they were closely associated were anarchism and later Bolshevism [a set of political beliefs associated with Communist Russia]. As in the case of contemporary political violence, or even the radical Islamism supported by a minority of British Muslims, anarchism and Bolshevism only commanded minority support among the Jewish community. But shared countries of origin and a common ethnic and religious background were enough to create a racialised discourse whenever there were anarchist outrages in London in the early 20th century.

Most anarchists were peaceful, but a few resorted to violent attacks such as the bombing of Greenwich Observatory in 1894—described at the time as an "international terrorist outrage". Anarchist violence was an international phenomenon. In Europe it claimed hundreds of lives, including those of several heads of government, and resulted in anti-terrorism laws. In the siege of Sidney Street in London in 1911, police and troops confronted east European Jewish anarchists. This violent confrontation in the heart of London created a racialised moral panic in which the whole Jewish community was stigmatised. It was claimed that London was "seething" with violent aliens, and the British establishment was said to be "in a state of denial". East End Jews were said to be "alienated", not "integrated", and a "threat to our security" a long time before anyone dreamed up the phrase "Londonistan".

Compare Historical Treatment of Jews to That of Muslims

Today the Middle East is the focus of a challenge to American political and economic hegemony, which is being presented as a "civilisational conflict with Islam". Nearly a century ago, the Russian revolution sent shockwaves through western states and financial markets. Anti-semites argued that Jewish involvement in revolutionary politics was part of a conspiracy by "the homeless wandering Jew" to replace European states with their "Hebrew nation". [Former British prime minister] Winston Churchill, as secretary of state for war in 1920, wrote an article in the *Illustrated Sunday Herald* claiming there were three categories of Jews—

The graves of Muslim servicemen in France have been desecrated by vandals painting Nazi swastikas on headstones.

good, bad and indifferent—and arguing that they were part of a "world-wide conspiracy for the overthrow of civilisation and for the reconstitution of society on the basis of arrested development".

Jews were the first non-Christian, yet monotheistic, religious minority in Britain. They are also one of its earliest "racialised" people. Despite important differences, the treatment of British Jews provides an illuminating comparison with contemporary anti-Muslim racism. There are recurring patterns in British society that racialise Jews and Muslims, which we need to understand if we are to develop an effective strategy for national security.

Jews and now Muslims have been and are the targets of cultural racism: differences arising from their religious culture are pathologised and systematically excluded from definitions of "being British". Both anti-semitism and anti-Muslim racism focus on belief in religious law to construct Jews and Muslims as a threat to the nation. Pnina Werbner, professor of social anthropology at Keele University, argues that Jews are predominantly racialised as an assimilated threat to national interests emerging at moments of crisis. Muslims are now being represented as a different kind of "folk devil"—a social group that is openly and aggressively trying to impose its religion on national culture. This partially explains the recent concerns about multiculturalism. "Anti-fundamentalist images provide racists with a legitimising discourse against Muslims," as Werbner puts it, which is used by "intellectual elites as well as 'real' violent racists".

Dangers of Lapsing into Stereotyping and Prejudice

The Jewish-Muslim comparison reveals another recurring pattern in recent British history: the rapid collapse of security fears associated with a religious minority into a racialised discourse of "civilisation versus barbarism". The American philosopher William Connolly predicted after September 11 that "the terrorism of al-Qaida, in turn, generates new fears and hostilities. The McCarthyism [a period of paranoia in the United States, centered around the fear of communism] of our day will connect internal state security to an exclusionary version of the Judeo-Christian tradition". . . . As Ken Macdonald, [British] director of public prosecutions warned, if we want to safeguard our security we must abandon delusions that we are fighting wars, and deal with terrorism in the context of criminal justice. With more terror arrests inevitable, and the prospect of new anti-terrorism legislation any day, the need to grasp what is really going on could not be more urgent.

EVALUATING THE AUTHOR'S ARGUMENTS:

In the viewpoint you just read, author Maleiha Malik begins by describing the characteristics of some British Jewish immigrants in the early twentieth century. However, Malik intends that the reader think of modern religious Muslim immigrants when reading the opening paragraph. In your opinion, is this an effective way to begin the essay? Think back to your reaction when you realized who Malik was actually writing about. Were you surprised or not? Why?

Anti-Semitism and Anti-Muslim Prejudice Should Not Be Compared

"There is no new wave of anti-Semitism in Western Europe . . . however, there is a rapidly rising tide of Islamophobia."

Gwynne Dyer

In the following viewpoint author Gwynne Dyer argues that anti-Semitism and anti-Muslim prejudice in Europe are not similar. In fact, Dyer writes, he believes there is no new anti-Semitism in Europe at all. Rather, Muslims are the ones being vilified by politicians and in the media and arts, including novels. This prejudice is far worse than any Jews experience, Dyer states, and is of much more concern. Because there are many Muslim immigrants to European countries, and they tend to be poor and uneducated, they make easy targets, in the author's opinion. Dyer is a journalist and lecturer based in London.

AS YOU READ, CONSIDER THE FOLLOWING QUESTIONS:

1. What is the connection between French political candidate Jean-Marie Le Pen and the anti-Semitism scare in Europe?
2. According to the author, what is the real reason American media continue to focus on the threat of anti-Semitism?
3. What is one reason provided by the author for the rising tide of "Islamophobia?"

Gwynne Dyer, "Europe Swamped by Rising Tide of Islamophobia," *New Zealand Herald*, June 10, 2002. Reproduced by permission.

"The most stupid religion is Islam," said best-selling French novelist Michel Houellebecq. In his [2001] novel, *Plateforme*, he has the narrator say: "Each time that I hear that a Palestinian terrorist, or a Palestinian child, or a pregnant Palestinian woman has been shot in the Gaza Strip, I shiver with enthusiasm at the thought that there is one less Muslim."

Houellebecq is a cynical poseur who would say anything to gain attention, but the problem is that many Europeans give him the attention he craves rather than shunning him. Yet what are we all being urged to worry about (especially by American political commentators)? Not about rampant *Islamophobia* in Europe, but rather about the alleged upsurge of *anti-Semitism* on the Continent.

The anti-Semitism scare was unleashed by National Front [a far-right political party] leader Jean-Marie Le Pen's surprise success in pushing the [left-wing] Socialist candidate into third place in the first round of the French presidential elections in April [2002]. But Le Pen is not a new Hitler; he is just an opportunistic political thug whose dismissive remarks about the Holocaust ("a detail of history") have never been forgotten or forgiven by the majority of French voters.

FAST FACT

According to the Human Rights Watch, hate crimes against Muslims in the United States rose by 1,700 percent in the months following the September 11 attacks.

In the run-off round of voting in May [2002] 82 percent of French voters held their noses and supported President Jacques Chirac despite his obvious corruption, rather than vote for the racist rabble-rouser Le Pen. As for the 18 percent who did back Le Pen, far more would have been motivated by their hatred and fear of immigrants (that is, Muslims) than of Jews.

Anti-Muslim Prejudice Is Rampant

So why, then, do the American media in particular continue to harp on the threat of resurgent anti-Semitism in Europe? Mainly because it serves as a convenient (if false) explanation for why European governments and peoples show much greater sympathy for the Palestinian cause than is normal in American official and media circles.

The reality is that the recent and unprecedented entry of far-right political parties into governing coalitions in a number of European countries is directly connected with rising popular resentment of immigrants, and that the majority of those immigrants almost everywhere are Muslims.

Look at the . . . inclusion of far-right parties in the Danish, Norwegian and Portuguese Governments: not an anti-Semitic word or hint in any of their campaigns. Look at the remarkable success of assassinated politician Pim Fortuyn's party in [the May 2002] Dutch election: he won his popularity by calling for an end to immigration

It has been suggested that anti-Muslim prejudice in Europe is tied to the rise in immigrants coming from the Middle East.

and referring to Islam as "a backward religion", but he never uttered a single word that suggested he harboured anti-Semitic views. Even Italy's Prime Minister Silvio Berlusconi, a right-wing populist who freely airs his anti-Muslim views, would never dream of saying anything anti-Semitic in public.

There are occasional anti-Semitic outrages in Europe—desecration of Jewish graveyards, daubing swastikas on synagogues and the like—because in a continent of 700 million people there are bound to be some malevolent fools. The recent increase in these incidents is probably due to the fact that some Muslims resident in Europe have picked up the anti-Semitic ideas that once flourished on the Continent, but are alien to traditional Islamic cultures.

Reasons for the Upsurge in Anti-Muslim Prejudice

But there is no new wave of anti-Semitism in Western Europe, and it is no worse in Eastern Europe than it was 10 years ago.

In all of Europe, however, there is a rapidly rising tide of Islamophobia: politicians capitalising on popular dislike of Muslim immigrants, and even outright vilification of Islam. It is no worse than the routine public vilification of infidels and their satanic creeds by Islamic extremists that goes unrebuked in many of the world's Muslim countries, but that is no excuse for Europeans to behave the same way.

Why is it happening? Part of the reason is the sheer number of Muslim immigrants. Whether it's Turks in Germany, Algerians and Moroccans in France, or Bangladeshis and Pakistanis in Britain, Muslims occupy the same dominant position in immigration flows to Western Europe that Latin Americans do in the United States, so they tend to become the targets for anti-immigrant hostility in general. Coming mostly from poor, rural areas of their old countries, they also tend to end up at the bottom of the socio-economic heap in their new ones, and poor people make easy victims.

Fear of and Cruelty Toward Muslims

There is also an ancestral memory in Western European cultures of a time when the Muslims of the Middle East were a powerful and terrifying enemy. None of this old history has much real relevance today, but it is still there for unscrupulous politicians and attention-seeking journalists to exploit.

So we have, for example, the case of Oriana Fallaci, formerly a well-known war correspondent and always a relentless self-promoter, who at the age of 72 has found a new hobby-horse to ride. [In] December [2001] she published a book called *Anger and Pride* in which she denounced Europeans who sympathise with the Palestinian cause as anti-Semites "who would sell their own mothers to a harem in order to see Jews once again in the gas chambers".

Percentage of Muslims in European Countries, 2005

Percent of Total Population that Is Muslim

- 0–0.99 percent
- 1–1.99 percent
- 2–3.99 percent
- 4–5.99 percent
- 6–7.99 percent
- 8–9.99 percent
- Largest sources of Muslim immigrants

Taken from: Dow Jones & Co., "Europe's Muslim Communities," 2005.

Her pro-Israeli stance, however, is only a pretext for an attack on Muslims: "Vile creatures who urinate in baptistries" and "multiply like rats". The book is in its fifth printing in Italy and has also become a best-seller in Spain. It is [being] published in France and stands to do even better than Houellebecq's filth.

EVALUATING THE AUTHOR'S ARGUMENTS:

In the viewpoint you just read, author Gwynne Dyer quotes a character from a novel by Michel Houellebecq. The character harbors anti-Muslim prejudice. Dyer uses this quote to support his argument that Islamophobia is on the upswing in Europe. Do you think that use of the Houellebecq quote adds to or detracts from Dyer's argument? How is a quote from a fictional character different from a quote from a politician or a public figure?

Chapter 2

How Should Jews View the Holocaust?

Walls of photographs memorialize the Holocaust at the U.S. Holocaust Museum in Washington, D.C.

The Holocaust Could Happen Again

"Having failed in the universalist attempt to prevent genocides . . . we are now facing a turning back of the clock to the 1930s. . . . And at the epicenter of this threat stands the Jewish people."

The Jerusalem Post

In the following viewpoint the editors of the Israeli English-language newspaper the *Jerusalem Post* argue that there is a very real possibility that another Holocaust could occur. Despite the mistakes of the past, genocides of other ethnic groups are currently happening, the editors write, despite the efforts of the UN and other humanitarian organizations. Jews are not immune from this threat. According to the authors, the country of Iran poses a serious threat to the Jewish people and the state of Israel. The president of Iran wants to lead a genocide against Jews, the editors state, and he must be stopped so that history will not repeat itself.

AS YOU READ, CONSIDER THE FOLLOWING QUESTIONS:

1. What is the meaning of the phrase "universalist cry" as used in the viewpoint?
2. According to the viewpoint, what is the ultimate goal of Iranian president Mahmoud Ahmadinejad?
3. What action does the author suggest Western nations take against Iran as an alternative to a military attack?

"Never Again," *The Jerusalem Post*, April 15, 2007, p. 13.

[As] Holocaust Memorial Day begins [on April 16, 2007], we remember the six million Jews who were systematically murdered by Nazi Germany. As we do so, it is not just the passage of time that makes it difficult to imagine the enormity of this crime, the suffering of the victims, and the implications for the human condition.

Since the Holocaust the Jewish people—already commanded to remember its long history—has become obsessed with commemorating an atrocity greater than the many it had already experienced. Holocaust museums have become ubiquitous as Jews have rightly argued that this crime cannot be viewed merely through the narrow lens of anti-Semitism but must be seen as a challenge to all peoples and to all future generations.

FAST FACT

By 1945, two out of every three European Jews had been killed in the Holocaust, according to the United States Holocaust Memorial Museum.

The challenge is expressed in the resonating words: Never again. It is this challenge that animated the founding institutions and concepts of the post-war international order—the United Nations, the Genocide Convention, the Universal Declaration of Human Rights, the notion of war criminals and their prosecution.

But these institutions and the nations behind them failed to prevent genocides in Cambodia and Rwanda and massacres and ethnic cleansing in Bosnia and are now failing in Darfur. The universalist cry "never again" rings hollow.

Modern-Day Genocides Are Occurring

The Committee of Conscience, a body established by the council that oversees the US Holocaust Memorial Museum in Washington, has categorized current humanitarian crises according to urgency. The committee has issued a "watch" on the situation in Chechnya and since 2004 an "emergency" (meaning that "acts of genocide or related crimes against humanity are occurring or immediately threatened") regarding Darfur.

It is of course more than appropriate for Holocaust museums to see their role not just in terms of displaying the past but affecting the present and the future. Last month [March 2007], Yad Vashem [the Jerusalem Holocaust memorial] took Sudanese refugees in Israel on a special tour of the museum. "People were supposed to learn from history," one of them responded. "But still it happens now. In 1994 in Rwanda and now in Darfur. I thought the world was supposed to learn."

In this vein, just after the Iranian regime hosted Holocaust deniers in Teheran [on December 11, 2006], Yad Vashem convened a briefing for the diplomatic corps titled "Holocaust Denial: Paving the Way to Genocide." Yad Vashem Chairman Avner Shalev explained Iranian President Mahmoud Ahmadinejad has made Holocaust denial part of a strategic agenda; not an academic or intellectual issue. Ahmadinejad wants to lead an Islamic jihad and to orchestrate another genocide aimed at destroying the State of Israel.

The creation of the Magyar Garda *(Hungarian Guard) by an extreme-right political party has led many to be concerned about a rise in anti-Semitism.*

Keeping Remembrance Strong

This chart shows the percentage of people in various nations who support keeping remembrance of the Holocaust strong.

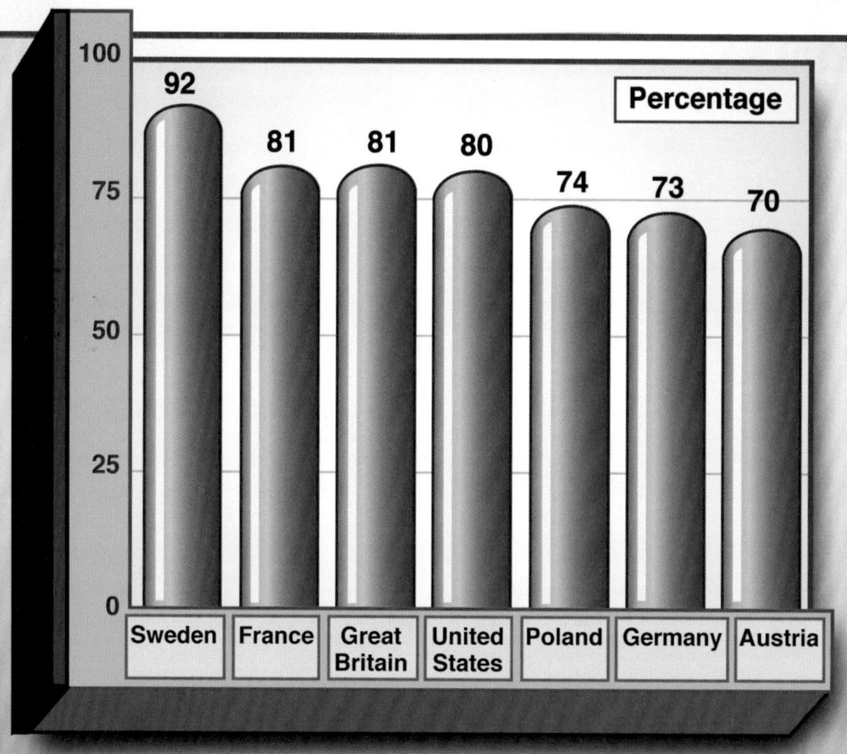

Taken from: American Jewish Committee, "AJC Survey Shows Commitment to Preserving Holocaust Memory," May 4, 2005. www.ajc.org.

At this event Yosef (Tommy) Lapid, a Holocaust survivor and former justice minister who now chairs Yad Vashem's council said, "If Europe missed the opportunity to understand what Hitler was promising, then Europe should believe what the Iranian president is saying now. He means business. The entire Judeo-Christian tradition is in a battle for survival against radical Islam."

Avoid Another Holocaust

Seven years into the 21st century the situation is this: Having failed in the universalist attempt to prevent genocides and war crimes in Asia, Africa and even in the heart of Europe, and failing now to stop a genocide in Darfur, we are now facing a turning back of the clock to the 1930s in which new tyrants threaten both genocide and world war. And once again at the epicenter of this threat stands the Jewish people.

It is not too late to stop Iran. The mullahs, beset by bitter and growing opposition at home and by internal power struggles, cannot withstand a full diplomatic and economic boycott imposed by Western nations. It still may be possible to avoid the need for military action.

What is abundantly clear however is that jihadist Iran, like Nazi Germany, will not stop until it is stopped. As in the 1930s, a refusal now to employ sufficient nonmilitary means to confront megalomaniacal tyrants now will not avoid war but precipitate it.

The Jewish people must not flinch from sounding this alarm. To paraphrase the sage Hillel, if not the Jews, then who? And if not now, then when?

EVALUATING THE AUTHOR'S ARGUMENTS:

Using the information provided, evaluate this quote from the viewpoint you just read: "'If Europe missed the opportunity to understand what Hitler was promising, then Europe should believe what the Iranian president is saying now. He means business. The entire Judeo-Christian tradition is in a battle for survival against radical Islam.'" Do you agree or disagree with this statement? Give your reasons using evidence from the viewpoint.

Viewpoint 2

The Holocaust Could Never Happen Again

"There is a growing debate . . . about whether the external threats to the Jewish community worldwide are similar to those just before the outbreak of World War II. The challenges now facing world Jewry . . . are not remotely similar."

Stuart Eizenstat

Stuart Eizenstat is a former American ambassador to the European Union and was President Bill Clinton's special representative on Holocaust-era issues. In the following viewpoint Eizenstat argues that despite the active threat of anti-Semitism, modern Jewry does not face a similar situation to that of 1938, the year just before the outbreak of World War II and the start of the Holocaust. The existence of the state of Israel is a prime difference, providing a place of refuge for all Jews. In addition, Eizenstat writes, the world community is far more sensitive and responsive to threats to Israel and Jews than it ever was early in the twentieth century.

AS YOU READ, CONSIDER THE FOLLOWING QUESTIONS:

1. Summarize the three reasons given by the author that challenges facing Jews today are different from those immediately before World War II.
2. According to the author, what is the major external challenge to Jews in the United States?
3. What are two external threats to Israel as identified by the author?

Stuart Eizenstat, "The Dangers Are Great, but It Is Not 1938," *Forward*, April 20, 2007. Reproduced by permission.

There is a growing debate within the American Jewish community about whether the external threats to the Jewish community worldwide are similar to those just before the outbreak of World War II. The challenges now facing world Jewry, however, are not remotely similar—because of the creation of the State of Israel, because of the lessons learned from the Holocaust, because of the integration of Jews into Western societies and, critically, because the most profound challenges facing Israel and world Jewry are shared by the wider world.

To act on the proposition that the threats today are equivalent to those in 1938 would lead to inappropriate and counterproductive policy responses. Nevertheless, there are significant dangers now facing world Jewry. In 1938, Adolf Hitler had been in power for five years and had begun to apply anti-Jewish laws while planning the invasion of Europe. His "Final Solution" became official policy later, as a result of both his vehement antisemitism and the failure of the Allied powers to agree to take any additional Jewish refugees, a failure he took as a clear signal that the world's democracies put a low priority on saving Jewish lives.

In 1938, Palestine was still under the British Mandate, and there was no independent Jewish state to afford a refuge to Jews in danger. Public opinion polls in the United States showed some 40% of the American public held antisemitic stereotypes of Jews and that in Europe there was rampant antisemitism, much of it church-based. Hitler had a largely free hand in perpetrating the Holocaust, and indeed, in several Eastern European countries local residents facilitated the Nazi genocide. In France, a Vichy regime would soon be created that passed its own anti-Jewish laws and cooperated with German authorities to deport tens of thousands of French Jews to their deaths.

Israel's Existence Protects Jews

Today, however, there is a third Jewish commonwealth, a state that over the years has been a sanctuary for Jews in distress, from Arab nations to the former Soviet Union.

Israel has one of the world's five most powerful military capabilities. It can defend itself against any conventional attack. Israel has signed peace agreements with two of its most powerful foes, Egypt and Jordan, and they have been scrupulously followed. While it is not the warm peace we might have wished for, it is a peace nevertheless, and it takes pressure off Israel's military forces.

In 2002, and again [in 2007] . . . Saudi Arabia proposed a peace initiative, accepted by the entire Arab League, offering normalized relations with Israel. While the conditions are clearly unacceptable, the willingness to recognize Israel by some of its most vociferous foes is noteworthy. I likewise believe an agreement with Syria could be reached that protects Israel's security interests.

Moreover, while antisemitism has not been extinguished, the gravity of the Holocaust has been imbedded in world opinion. Levels of general antisemitic attitudes have declined sharply. There has been a successful decades-long Catholic-Jewish dialogue, with important statements by the Vatican that diminish religious-based antisemitism.

Indeed, intermarriage rates have soared in the United States and in Western Europe—a clear and present danger to Jewish continuity, to be sure, but a symbol of the acceptance of Jews by general society. Most Western European countries have Holocaust remembrance days, and several have Holocaust memorial museums, commemorations that were both initiated by the United States during the Carter administration.

While it is sad that it is needed, virtually every major European nation provides police protection for Jewish synagogues and religious schools. Antisemitic actions are met with firm responses, as in France, albeit belatedly. To its credit, the French anti-hate crimes law was amended to include antisemitic actions.

Jews Have Allies from Enemies

Our work during the Clinton administration raised the implications of the Holocaust back onto the world agenda, with belated justice for Holocaust victims and their families—some $8 billion in compensation and restitution overall. Of long-term significance, more than a dozen countries undertook official reviews of their role in misusing confiscated Jewish property, the most searching being the Swiss and French reports. And the Holocaust Education Task Force, initiated

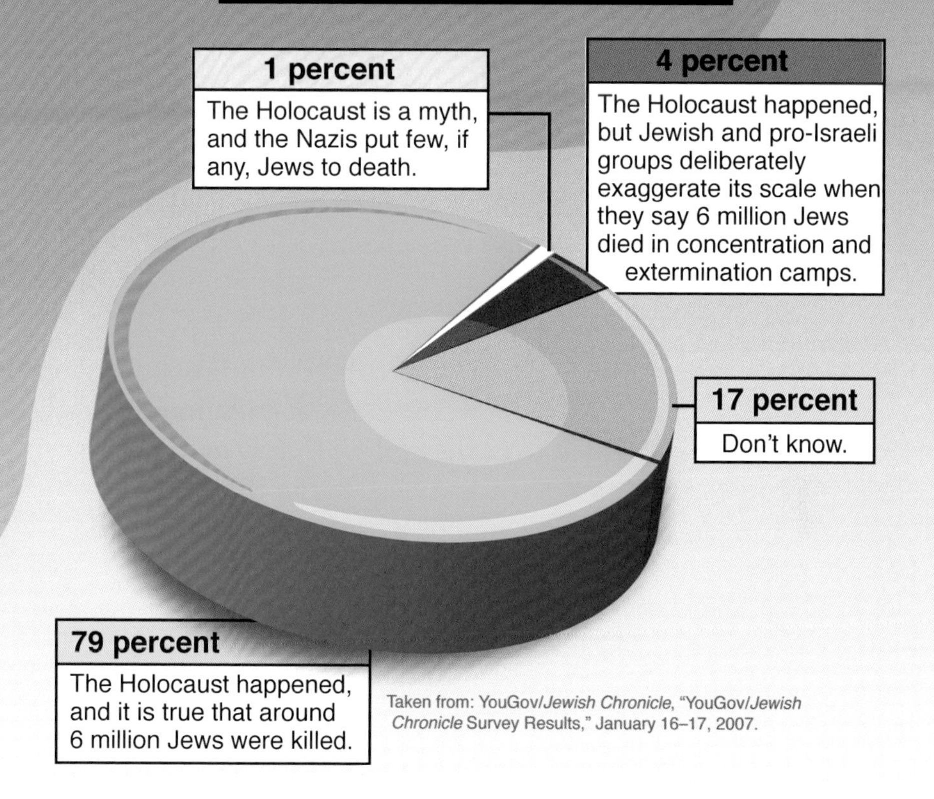

by Sweden and now including more than 20 nations, is promoting Holocaust education in school systems around the world, under the guidance of [the Holocast memorial] Yad Vashem in Israel. Likewise, the Jewish community in the United States, largely quiescent during World War II, has learned the lessons of its silence and has vowed "never again." Jewish organizations are active, public and vocal in defending Jewish interests both at home and abroad.

Yet there are genuine external threats to Jews around the world. The difference is that the Jewish people and Israel today have allies in combating those threats.

The major external challenge in the United States, beyond sporadic antisemitic incidents, is actually symbolic of the clout held by Jews in the American political arena: the canard that the so-called "Jewish lobby" controls American policy in the Middle East in ways that are disadvantageous to America's national security interests. There is a troubling growth of anti-Israel sentiment on American college campuses, stemming primarily from the Israeli occupation of territory captured in self-defense following the Six Day War.

There is a fine line—which is at times being disturbingly crossed—between legitimate criticism of Israeli government policy and the delegitimization of Israel as a Jewish state. But troubling as these incidents are, there is little resonance among the general American public, which by overwhelming numbers is supportive of Israel compared to the Arab world, even more so since the September 11 terrorist attacks.

Danger to Jews in Europe

European Jews face a situation of greater concern. In Europe, public opinion is sharply anti-Israel, with recent Eurostat polls finding Israel, along with the United States, to be the greatest threats to world peace, ahead of Iran, North Korea, Syria and Iraq. In the United Kingdom, one of the two largest academic unions passed a motion [in 2006] to boycott Israeli academic institutions.

Of even greater concern is the radicalization of a small-but-dangerous part of the European Muslim community, which was underscored by the tragic 2006 murder of [French Jew] Ilan Halimi in Paris. There are some 20 million Muslims in Europe today, with the number likely to grow to 50 million in the next 25 years. The overwhelming majority are peaceful and want a better way of life, but there may be a growing number of radicals at the fringe feeding on the Palestinian conflict and on the lack of jobs and education in their adopted homes in Europe.

European leaders, it must be noted, recognize the need to crack down on the radicals. The French Muslim riots in 2005, the bus and subway bombings in London the same year, and the train bombing in Madrid in 2004 were attacks on Western societies, not against Jews, and therefore elicited responses from political leaders to defend broader national interests. As the Islamic influence grows in Europe, leaders throughout key Western European nations are trying to fashion policies that better integrate Muslim immigrants into society while maintaining traditional European values. European Jews are not alone in facing the challenge of the Islamization of the European continent.

The external challenges facing American and European Jewry, however, pale in comparison with the external threats facing Israel—namely, the growth of Hamas in the Palestinian territories and of Hezbollah in Lebanon, and the rise of Iran, a major financial, spiritual and military

Some think that alliances between Israel and strong powers, like the United States, will prevent the large-scale violence against Jews that occurred during the Holocaust.

supporter of both radical groups. The United States and the European Union [E.U.] both list Hamas as a terrorist organization, and the diplomatic quartet of the United States, E.U., United Nations and Russia refuses to recognize Hamas until it recognizes Israel's right to exist, forswears violence and accepts all previous peace agreements. The United States takes the same position regarding Hezbollah. While both organizations are very troubling, neither is a threat to Israel's existence.

Jews Are Stronger Now

Iran is a different story. It poses a potential existential threat to Israel. Its president has vowed to wipe Israel off the map and denies the Holocaust, and the country has both a medium-range missile capacity and a voracious appetite for nuclear weapons. But again, Israel's concerns are widely shared.

Moderate, pro-Western Arab leaders are as concerned as Israel about the possibility that a nuclear-armed Shiite Iran will dominate the region and destabilize their regimes. Acting on findings by the

International Atomic Energy Agency, the United States has gotten strong support from the E.U. and from the U.N. Security Council for economic sanctions against Iran.

The view that it is unacceptable for a radicalized Iran to possess nuclear weapons is shared by Western nations, most Arab countries and even Russia. How Iran will be deterred remains to be seen. But what is critical to remember is that Israel is not isolated in its grave concerns, and should not unilaterally initiate military action at this time.

World Jewry and Israel do indeed face external problems. But it does no good to suggest that these problems are equivalent to those that an essentially weak Jewish community faced in 1938.

EVALUATING THE AUTHORS' ARGUMENTS:

In the viewpoint you just read, author Stuart Eizenstat argues that the existence of Israel and support of the world community make it unlikely that Jews will ever face a threat such as the Holocaust again. In the previous viewpoint, the editors of the *Jerusalem Post* argue that modern-day genocides demonstrate that the world has not learned from the mistakes of the past and that the Holocaust could occur in some form again. With which argument do you agree? Why?

Jews Should Keep Memories of the Holocaust Alive

"Remembering the Holocaust and encouraging others to remember it too has served a very positive end."

Martin Plax

Martin Plax is a professional mediator and associate professor of political science at Cleveland State University. In the following viewpoint Plax argues that Jews should not let the world forget the Holocaust. However, in light of a rise in anti-Semitism, Plax writes that current methods of remembering the Holocaust are not as effective as they could be. Jews should strive to not only evoke pity and compassion in others for the atrocities they suffered at the hands of the Nazis, but also to inspire charity and mercy. Combining remembrances with public action of some sort will help to achieve this end, Plax states.

AS YOU READ, CONSIDER THE FOLLOWING QUESTIONS:

1. According to the author, what has been the effect of the appropriation by different groups of the label "Nazi?"
2. What kind of people in general do we pity, according to the author?
3. According to the author, what would be a more constructive way of remembering the Holocaust?

For decades it appeared that regular reminders of the horrors of the Holocaust made public expressions of anti-Semitism and acts of hatred against Jews impermissible. Believing that this situation would continue, some Jewish writers . . . began to criticize the Jewish community's seeming dependence on the Holocaust, on the grounds that it provided only negative reasons for Jewish identity. They argued that Judaism has a raison d'être [reason for existence] grounded in the positive and that these should be accentuated. The . . . resurgence of anti-Semitism in Europe and North America, compounding the murders of innocent Israelis by suicide bombers, however has challenged the belief that civility towards Jews would last indefinitely. Those hate-driven acts make it imperative to consider if regular public recollections of the Holocaust have not reached a point of diminishing returns.

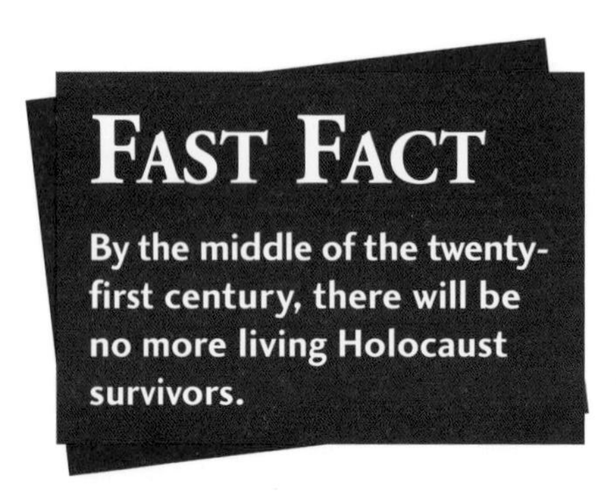

During my nearly twenty-six years of experience as Cleveland director of [the nonprofit organization] The American Jewish Committee, I had steady contacts with other religious and nationality communities in the Greater Cleveland area. Through those experiences I learned that even people sensitive to Nazi atrocities are not made more sympathetic to Jews simply by sharing their stories of atrocities against their people. They believe that by insisting that Nazi atrocities were sui generis [unique in their characteristics], the Jewish community is using a double standard when it comes to what constitutes war crimes. The one thing that did promote civility and a willingness to support Jewish interests was for us to engage in acts that signaled the feelings of mutual gratitude. . . .

Hurtful Labels Are Being Misused

There can be little doubt that the stigma of being called a Nazi is real. But the term Nazi, like the word Holocaust, has been appropriated by nearly every group wishing to call attention to its own plight. Analogies from the language of the Holocaust are being made. Israel has been called a Nazi-state and Prime Minister Ariel Sharon has been compared to Hitler. In spite of protests from Jews, in reality, no one using these egregious comparisons has been deterred. The contrary has taken place. Sensing that the Jewish community feels vulnerable because of those charges, the perpetrators appear to be taking comfort in the Jewish responses. . . .

At a time when anti-Semitism is being expressed publicly, both in word and deed, and the language of the Holocaust is being turned against Israel and the Jewish community, one has to wonder if something should be done about the way the Holocaust is remembered.

Holocaust Deaths

Country/Region	Low Estimate	High Estimate
Germany (1938 borders)	125,000	130,000
Austria	58,000	65,000
Belgium and Luxembourg	24,700	29,000
Bulgaria	0	7,000
Czechoslovakia	245,000	277,000
France	64,000	83,000
Greece	58,000	65,000
Hungary and Ukraine	300,000	402,000
Italy	7,500	8,000
Netherlands	101,800	106,000
Norway	677	760
Poland and USSR	3,700,000	4,565,000
Romania	40,000	220,000
Yugoslavia	54,000	60,000
Total	**4,778,677**	**6,017,760**

Taken from: Statistics derived from Yad Vashem and Gerald Fleming, *Hitler and the Final Solution.*

The idea that the Holocaust would serve as the grounds of moral instruction rests on the premise that morality can be continuously taught by encouraging humans to experience the pain suffered by other humans. The experience would induce a sense of pity, because it gave rise to compassion. . . . If people will realize the pain suffered by Jews at the hands of Nazis and their Jew-hating civilian sympathizers, they will contain, if not totally set aside whatever anti-Jewish prejudices they have and not just tolerate Jews but live with Jews in mutual freedom.

Pity Occurs When Harm Is Unjustified

Perhaps there is something about pity that has been forgotten and which needs to be remembered too. I was unexpectedly reminded of it when, during the Lenten season [the forty days before Easter] of 1987, I attended a performance of Tetelestai, a musical version of the Passion Play, at the request of the director of the Interfaith Commission of the Catholic Diocese of Cleveland.

Soon after the drama began, I was dissolved in the characters and their dialogue, especially in the character of Jesus, who was portrayed as a man within human reach. His words were familiar to me because of my reading of the New Testament but even more because he taught his followers "to love the Lord with all your soul and all your might." These are the words I repeat everyday as part of my Jewish obligation to repeat, with sincerity, the words of the Sh'ma ("Hear, O Israel! The Lord is God, the Lord is One").

So enthralled was I in the play that I didn't expect what happened to me emotionally when I witnessed the crucifixion. As the cross was on the ground and the nails were being hammered into flesh and timber, my pulse started racing. I was growing uncomfortable and squirmed several times. No position gave me relief. Then, as the cross was slowly raised for all to see, I could feel anger raging inside of me.

The experience of anger made me wonder about the passion of pity. The more I thought of my own experience, the more it became clear that we pity only those people whose pain is, for us, unjustified. Who are they? People we believe are good or innocent. Pity, then, is a passion that is aroused because the harm done was unjust. It is the injustice that, when it arouses pity, also arouses anger.

Members of Hungary's Jewish community hold pictures from the Holocaust while demonstrating at the swearing-in ceremony of the Magyar Garda.

Pity, when aroused, may even arouse a suspicion that being "good" does not necessarily protect one from undeserved harm. If while his suspicion is aroused, someone identifies the cause of the injustice to the innocent person whom a person pities, the anger over the injustice evokes another passion: a desire for revenge. Among the memories of some European Jews is that in some places, Good Friday was a day when pogroms occurred.

Difficulty Comprehending Evil of the Holocaust

What is required to transform an initial rush of anger based on pity, from a desire for revenge into an emotional state that inspires self-sacrifice and public-spiritedness or altruism? An answer can be found in the emotions evoked for Christians at Easter and of Jews at Yom Kippur, (and I suspect among Muslims during Ramadan)—a sense of gratitude. It is a merciful God who saves us, physically and spiritually. Mercy, ironically, is a form of injustice, since the recipients of mercy get more than they deserve. When a person who is not morally depraved recognizes he or she has been the recipient of an act of mercy, or in human terms, charity, they are most likely to feel a sense of gratitude.

I mention the phrase "morally depraved" as a way of returning to the subject of the Holocaust and of today's expressions of hatred. The continuous fascination with the Holocaust, in spite of the many historical studies of events that occurred during that period, seems to be driven by our inability to comprehend how such a murderous regime could have conceived of and carried out its genocidal practices. It is not accidental that the language used about the Holocaust speaks of evil and moral depravity, that is, the language of religion. It is almost as uncanny as the experience of religious revelation. . . .

Memory Must Be Combined with Action

There is a risk of "remembering the past." But also, there is no way of avoiding it. I have always been mindful of a footnote in an essay I read many years ago on the Holocaust. It quoted Heinrich Himmler, who, at a Nazi Party meeting in 1942 said that the goal of the Nazis was to convince the entire German population that there was no such thing as a "decent Jew." If the program of extermination were ever to be a total success, it would require an attack on the very idea of decency. It was also an attack on any claim of individuality, that "this person is different because he is decent." "Decency" gets in the way of prejudices on an individual level. One gets a sense that there is another element in defining moral depravity: it is the purposeful destruction of the idea of decency.

Nowhere have I experienced the difference between people capable of accepting me as a decent Jew than when I have heard the phrase, "you're different." What do people mean when they say to a member of any disliked group, "you're different"? Given today's sensitivities, it is interpreted as an insult. But is it? The statement is meant as a compliment. It is a statement by a person who acknowledges having a prejudice but not being so blinded by that prejudice that he or she can't tell the difference between decent and indecent character in people, especially among those who belong to a group about whom he or she holds the prejudice. . . .

My experiences suggest that a more constructive notion of moral instruction is to encourage remembering with others, but with the goal of leading to some public action that demonstrates that each community truly appreciates the meaning that those memories have for the other community. Such activities can provide everyone with an incentive to make efforts to contain the harmful effects of the morally depraved that reside in every community. . . .

Remembering the Holocaust in a Different Way

Jews in America will likely continue to insist on remembering the Holocaust as a sui generis event in the history of the 20th century and continue to try to morally instruct the rest of the world in memory of those who were murdered in the Holocaust. But we run the risk that those we wish to instruct will continue to believe Jewish justice is undifferentiated from vengeance. I believe that it is necessary to modify that pursuit by engaging in actions that demonstrate that Judaism, like Christianity, not only teaches charity and gratitude, but also compels us to promote both. Doing the latter, the Jewish community would be taken more seriously when they say of the Holocaust, "forgive, but don't forget."

Remembering the Holocaust and encouraging others to remember it too has served a very positive end. But simply repeating those memories may not, any longer, insure that anyone will continue to learn from them about how to maximize the chances that the rules comprising the Noahidic code [a set of laws that all non-Jews are compelled to follow, according to ancient Jewish tradition] will continue to be followed.

EVALUATING THE AUTHOR'S ARGUMENTS:

Author Martin Plax believes that Jews should not allow memories of the Holocaust to die. However, he states, memory must be combined with actions by Jews that promote charity and gratitude. This will inspire others to have more sympathy for Jews who experience prejudice. Do you agree or disagree with this idea? Is it necessary for Jews to act, or should simply remembering the Holocaust be enough?

Jews Are Exploiting Memories of the Holocaust

"[My book] . . . posited a distinction between the Nazi holocaust—the systematic extermination of Jews during World War II—and The Holocaust—the instrumentalization of the Nazi holocaust by American Jewish elites and their supporters."

Norman Finkelstein

In the following viewpoint DePaul University political science professor Norman Finkelstein argues that Jews, especially American Jews, have used the trauma of the Holocaust to their own benefit, creating a "Holocaust Industry." They have created a separate "Holocaust" from that of the actual Nazi holocaust, Finkelstein writes. Jews are a powerful, elite group of people, Finkelstein writes. It is abuse of this power, he argues, that has brought on much of the current anti-Semitism in the world. Jews are not victims, the author argues, and they should not treat themselves as such. Norman Finkelstein is the author of several books about Jewish issues, including *The Holocaust Industry.*

AS YOU READ, CONSIDER THE FOLLOWING QUESTIONS:

1. According to the author, under what guise do American Jewish organizations seek to "blackmail Europe?"

Norman Finkelstein, "The Occupation's Spillover Effect," *Tikkun*, vol. 20, March/April 2005, pp. 13–14.

2. How many films has Hollywood produced on the Holocaust since 1989?
3. According to the author, who are the primary fomenters of anti-Semitism today?

Jews now rank as the wealthiest ethnic group in the United States; with this economic power has accrued substantial political power. Their leaders have wielded this power often crudely, to mold U.S. policy regarding Israel. These leaders have also utilized this power in other realms. Under the guise of seeking "Holocaust reparations," American Jewish organizations and individuals at all levels of government and in all sectors of American society entered into a conspiracy—this is the correct word—to blackmail Europe. . . .

And who can seriously believe that the pro-Jewish bias of the corporate media has nothing whatever to do with the influential Jewish presence at all levels of it? "It's undoubtedly true that there are prominent Jews among the producers, directors, studio executives, and stars in Hollywood," [Abraham H.] Foxman [director of the nonprofit Anti-Defamation League] concedes. "It's even true that, proportionately, there has always been a relatively prominent Jewish presence in the movie, TV, and record industries." But, he continues, "The Jews who work in Hollywood are there not as Jews but as actors, directors, writers, business executives, or what have you," concerned only with "the bottom line." His proof? "This explains the paradox that no anti-Semitic conspiracy theorist has ever tackled—how it is that the supposedly Jewish-controlled movie industry has produced so few films dealing with overtly Jewish characters or themes." Is that why Hollywood has produced a mere 175 films on The Holocaust since 1989?

Jews Behaving "as Jews"

Legitimate questions can surely be posed regarding when and if Jews are acting as people who happen to be Jewish or acting "as Jews," and, on the latter occasions (which plainly do arise), regarding the actual breadth and limits of this "Jewish power," but these questions can only be answered empirically, not a priori [based on deduction]

Governor Arnold Schwarzenegger receives a Holocaust Remembrance award. Some believe that the Holocaust is used to gain sympathy and support for the Jewish cause.

with politically correct formulae. To foreclose inquiry on this topic as anti-Semitic is, intentionally or not, to shield Jews from legitimate scrutiny of their uses and abuses of formidable power. In an otherwise sensible treatment of the new anti-Semitism, [author] Brian King [in his book *Patterns of Prejudice*] maintains that "it is a form of anti-Semitism" if an accusation against Jews mimics an anti-Semitic stereotype such as the idea of Jews being "powerful, wealthy . . . pursuing [their] own selfish ends." Yet, if Jews act out a Jewish stereotype, it plainly doesn't follow that they can't be committing the stereotypical act. Can't they commit a [negative] act even if it conforms to a Jewish stereotype? It is perhaps politically incorrect to recall, but nonetheless a commonplace, that potent stereotypes, like good propaganda, acquire their force from containing a kernel—and sometimes even more than a kernel—of truth. . . .

Jews Have Used the Holocaust for Their Own Gain

In [my 2000 book] *The Holocaust Industry*, [I] posited a distinction between the Nazi holocaust—the systematic extermination of Jews during World War II—and The Holocaust—the instrumentalization of the Nazi holocaust by American Jewish elites and their supporters. A parallel distinction needs to be made between anti-Semitism—the unjustifiable targeting of Jews solely for being Jews—and "anti-Semitism"—the instrumentalization of anti-Semitism by American (or other) Jewish elites. Like The Holocaust, "anti-Semitism" is an ideological weapon to deflect justified criticism of Israel and, concomitantly, powerful Jewish interests. In its current usage, "anti-Semitism," alongside the "war against terrorism," serves as a cloak for a massive assault on international law and human rights. Those Jews committed to the struggle against the real anti-Semitism must, in the first instance, expose this specious "anti-Semitism" for the sham it is. "[T]here are no patent remedies and quick solutions available" for anti-Semitism, the authors of *Manifestations* conclude. "[I]t is not possible to formulate a once and for all strategy, which is effective everywhere." This writer begs to differ. Tell the truth, fight for justice: this is the time-tested strategy for fighting anti-Semitism, as well as other forms of bigotry. If, as all the important studies agree, current resentment against Jews has coincided with Israel's brutal repression of the Palestinians, then a patent remedy and quick solution would plainly be to end the occupation. A full Israeli withdrawal would also deprive those real anti-Semites exploiting Israel's repression as a pretext to demonize Jews—and who can doubt they exist?—of a dangerous weapon as well as expose their real agenda. And, the more vocally Jews dissent from Israel's occupation, the fewer will be those non-Jews who mistake Israel's criminal policies and the uncritical support (indeed encouragement) of mainline Jewish organizations for the popular Jewish mood.

Fast Fact

The Nazis sent groups other than Jews to the concentration camps, including political protesters, the disabled, Romany people (also called Gypsies), Jehovah's Witnesses, and gays and lesbians.

Talking About the Holocaust

This chart shows the percentage of Europeans who responded that it is "probably true" that Jews talk too much about the Holocaust.

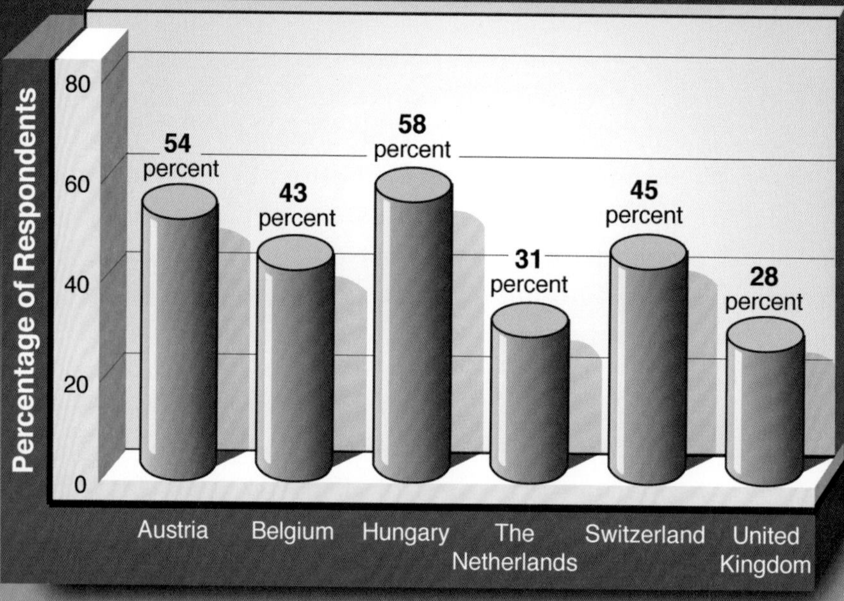

Taken from: Anti-Defamation League, "Attitudes Toward Jews and the Middle East in Six European Countries," July 2007. www.adl.org.

The Holocaust Industry Contributes to Anti-Semitism

On the other side, the worst enemies in the struggle against real anti-Semitism are the philo-Semites [those who love, rather than hate Jews or Semites]. This problem typically arises on the European scene. By turning a blind eye to Israeli crimes in the name of sensitivity to past Jewish suffering, they enable Israel to continue on a murderous path that foments anti-Semitism and, for that matter, the self-destruction of Israelis. The philo-Semitic application of this special dispensation to American Jewish elites has proven equally catastrophic. As already noted, Jewish elites in the United States have enjoyed enormous prosperity. From this combination of economic and political power has sprung, unsurprisingly, a mindset of Jewish superiority. Wrapping themselves in the mantle of The Holocaust, these Jewish elites pretend—and, in their own solipsistic universe, perhaps even imagine themselves—to be victims, dismissing any and all criticism as manifestations of "anti-Semitism." And, from this lethal brew of formidable power, chauvinistic arrogance, feigned (or imagined) victimhood, and Holocaust-immunity to criticism has sprung a terrifying recklessness and ruthlessness on the part of American Jewish elites. Alongside Israel, they are the main fomenters of anti-Semitism in the world today. Coddling them is not the answer. They need to be stopped.

EVALUATING THE AUTHOR'S ARGUMENTS:

In the viewpoint you just read, author Norman Finkelstein is very critical of modern Jews as a people, stating, among other things, that they have "wrapped themselves in the mantle of the Holocaust," deliberately exploiting memories of the Holocaust for their own gain. Norman Finkelstein is himself an American Jew. Does knowing his religious identity influence your opinion of his argument? Why or why not?

Chapter 3

What Issues Affect Modern Judaism?

The Conservative Judaism movement feels that it is important to maintain traditional commitments to Jewish life but also allows for some changes to their belief structure.

Intermarriage Is a Serious Problem for Jews

"It's my responsibility to keep it real—to perpetuate and strengthen the line of whatever the Jewish people can nobly contribute to this world."

Alexa Witt

In the following viewpoint author Alexa Witt writes about her personal decision not to intermarry. Marrying a Jew, Witt states, ensures continuity of the Jewish people and their heritage. Witt describes personal examples of those who have converted to Judaism from another religion in order to get married and states her belief that those conversions are at risk of failing. But far from limiting her options, states Witt, deciding to marry only a Jew has provided more of an opportunity to find her soul mate. Alexa Witt is a writer and columnist who addresses topics of Jewish identity and experience.

AS YOU READ, CONSIDER THE FOLLOWING QUESTIONS:

1. What are three questions the author asked herself after deciding to look seriously into what being Jewish meant to her?
2. Define "bashert."
3. Why was it important to the author's mother to maintain a vital Jewish people?

Alexa Witt, "Ma's Intermarriage Game," *Aish HaTorah,* December 4, 2005. Reproduced by permission.

When we were growing up, my mother would play a little brainwashing game with us. Funny, semi-ridiculous, it had a serious, explicit goal—to train us against marrying out.

"There are only two men left on the planet, and you have to marry one of them," Ma would say. The first guy's name was always Christopher. He was handsome, wealthy, crazy about me and treated me like a queen. The second guy was not particularly good-looking, poor, just as in love with me, but couldn't afford nice presents, and Jewish. "So who do you pick?"

An obvious set-up, half a joke, half not. The Game had only one right answer. Ma wouldn't let it end until we picked the Jew. Imagine floating on the yacht with Christopher, crystal blue waters twinkling in the sun. . . . Imagine life with the Jewish guy, drab green living room and no place to go. . . .

Arguments for conversion would be countered with real-life scare-stories of insincere conversions gone awry. Our cousin's friend, whose wife converted to marry him, then shortly after the man died, had all the kids baptized. The family friend whose non-Jewish wife became a Jesus freak and sent the kids to an evangelical summer camp from which they returned asking Daddy if he was Satan.

We would point out happily married, normal couples we knew where one spouse had converted to Judaism, but the basic message was clear: We were expected to marry a Jew, or someone who had converted out of a sincere desire to be Jewish.

FAST FACT

A non-Jew who converts to Judaism for marriage must satisfy three requirements for men, two for women: immersion in a ritual bath, an understanding of Jewish law, and, for men, circumcision.

Deciding Between Two Religions

Aside from the decidedly un-PC Game, we were brought up to believe that people of all races and religions are unique and important.

Still, our heads would be buzzing with visions of gorgeous, rich Christopher or supermodel Christina. To heighten the drama, my brothers and I would make the Jewish candidate extra-unattractive. "And the Jewish guy has a congenital drooling problem, right?"

We were testing Ma to see under what conditions she would finally cave in and say, "Okay, fine, you can marry the non-Jew." Instead, Ma would laugh at us and insist that, of course, we shouldn't be embarrassed or turned off by our spouses. The point was to consider and then overcome superficial, less important temptations. While Christopher and Christina could provide as much love, respect and companionship

Some Jews feel that marrying other Jews is the best way to preserve their culture and heritage.

as a Jewish spouse, they could never give the home a strong enough sense of Jewishness to pass onto the next generation.

Examining Jewish Marriage

This was all cute and theoretical until my brothers and I began attending university. Opportunities with real-life Christophers and Christinas abounded. One brother seriously dated a non-Jew for five years and considered marriage against our parents' wishes.

As for me, I was midstream American, doing everything a non-Jew would do . . . except marry one. And this seemed to be a real contradiction.

I decided I had to seriously look into what being Jewish meant to me. Why is it important to maintain Jews into future generations? Why is my participation essential rather than elective? And why does that mean that otherwise nice, liberal Jewish girls have to practice a form of "discrimination" in their personal lives?

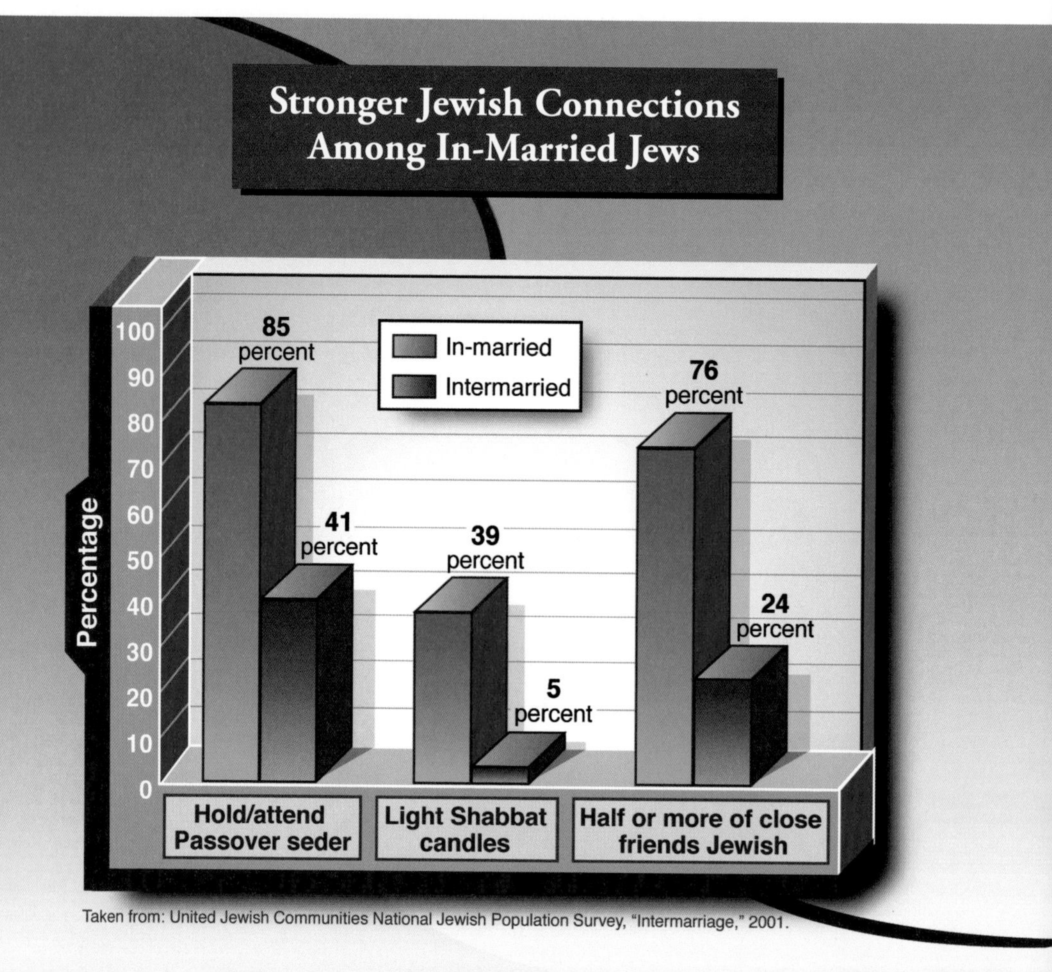

Taken from: United Jewish Communities National Jewish Population Survey, "Intermarriage," 2001.

I found a Jewish learning program where I was free to ask my questions, however sacrilegious. The young mentors there made an impact on me. Here were people my age I could relate to, approachable and normal, taking Judaism seriously, with an attitude of joy. I was impressed by their commitment to refinement through mitzvot [good deeds], integrating spirituality into physical life. Although it was Jewish culture and not religion that Ma had in mind in terms of continuity, I was interested in exploring the original source of the kitsch and sentimentality.

The bashert [a Yiddish word meaning destiny] concept was attractive: one predestined soul mate, announced in heaven before birth to be meant just for me. But his necessarily being Jewish sounded suspiciously familiar. . . . Because when being a link in a chain 2,000 years old is weighed against a personal desire for romance with whoever you want, it seems like a big old drag. If me and Christopher make each other happy, what's worth standing in the way of that?

Um, 2,000 years of history and culture, maybe? A niggling feeling that would never go away, that I'd be walking a plank and ending the Jewish people at me?

But is that just cliché Jewish guilt? Did I even have the ability to consciously choose my own values, or had I been hopelessly brainwashed by the Game?

When existential questioning approaches the [Jewish filmmaker] Woody Allen level, I stop to appreciate how Jewish I really am.

Deciding to Marry Jewish

Ultimately, it came down to valuing my Jewish identity so much that I knew it had to factor into life's most important decision, who to marry. If I were out strictly for my own self, I could easily be the end of the Jewish line. And I could not live with that.

In Ma's Game, marrying the Jew was the conciliatory decision, made out of obligation and not desire. When the Game became relevant in real life and I was forced to decide what my values were, my thinking underwent a switch. After the smoke cloud of heartbreak over Christopher cleared, there was left standing a woman proud of the responsibility to carry Jews on into the future.

Why is it so important to have a vital Jewish people? For Ma, it's about perpetuating a special people; all her parents' family was wiped out in the Holocaust, so she feels an urgent responsibility to keep the line going.

But these days, luckily, we don't feel that urgency. So, I ask, what's our raison d'etre [reason for existence]? And how is it that we shine so out of proportion to our numbers (one example: of the 25 billionaires in New York, 19 are Jewish)?

It must be because of what happened to us at Sinai, that mountain in the desert 3,000 years back. So if we've got the magic, then it's my responsibility to keep it real—to perpetuate and strengthen the line of whatever the Jewish people can nobly contribute to this world.

With this understanding, saying 'no' to Christopher became not a limitation but the most important opportunity in my life, freeing me up to find the guy who is everything I want—including Jewish. Luckily there weren't only *two* guys left in the world to marry—just *one*, the Jewish guy, the man who was meant for me.

EVALUATING THE AUTHOR'S ARGUMENTS:

The author of the viewpoint you just read, Alexa Witt, makes her argument against intermarriage by telling the story of her own decision to marry only another Jew. In your opinion, do her conversational style and personal details and memories work to convince you of her argument? Or would her points be better made in a more informative, analytical style? Why or why not?

Intermarriage Is Not Necessarily a Serious Problem for Jews

David G. Sacks

"Intermarrying Jews are . . . not per se rejecting either their heritage or their Jewishness."

David G. Sacks was a member of the Jewish Outreach Institute board and a former president of the Jewish Federation of New York. In the following viewpoint he argues that far from damaging Jewish identity, the increase in rates of intermarriage is actually evidence that Jews are stronger than ever. Jewish people have gained wide acceptance in the Gentile community since World War II, Sacks writes, and non-Jews are more willing to integrate Jews into their families. Since Jews are no longer segregated as they once were, they have more opportunities to meet spouses of other faiths.

AS YOU READ, CONSIDER THE FOLLOWING QUESTIONS:

1. According to the National Jewish Population Study cited in the article, what percent of Jews intermarried in 1985?
2. What are the three factors, according to the author, that account for the increase in intermarriage?
3. What are two factors that have helped change public views of the "Jewish stereotype?"

David G. Sacks, "You Are Not Alone, and Why Intermarriage Is Increasing," *Jewish Outreach Institute,* 2000. Reproduced by permission.

If yours is like the experience of most Jewish families, the first encounter with serious interfaith dating or intermarriage—typically through an adult child or grandchild—will bring on a keen sense of apartness. The long tradition of religious opposition, coupled with social stigma and the historical rarity of intermarriage among Jews, has made many Jewish families uneasy about the prospect of one of their own marrying someone who is not Jewish. The unspoken question, "Why is this happening to us?" is likely to gnaw at your thoughts for weeks or months.

[The] issue of intermarriage was brought more sharply to the entire Jewish community's attention by the Council of Jewish Federation's [now called United Jewish Communities] publication of the 1990 National Jewish Population Study. This study reported that in marriages involving Jews since 1985, about 52% were intermarriages. The 52% rate is probably now approaching 60%. Because each marriage involves two people, which means that three out of every four marriages involving American Jews are intermarriages. Whether we approve of this trend or not, it is, like the cycles of the sun or the tides, a fact. At present, there are about one million American households in which one adult is of Jewish background and the other is not.

Knowledge of this simple demographic fact, alone, should lessen some of the emotional turmoil that often attends the first intermarriage to occur in a modern Jewish family.

FAST FACT

According to a survey by the Central Conference of American Rabbis, 48 percent of rabbis in the Reform movement say they perform interfaith wedding ceremonies. The Conservative and Orthodox movements prohibit rabbis from officiating at weddings between Jews and non-Jews.

Reasons for the Intermarriage Increase

Intermarriage is increasingly common today among American Jews, as it is among all Americans, because of three factors, which were largely absent in prior generations: freedom, willingness, and acceptability. Unlike the situation fifty years ago, with many neighborhoods, areas, and buildings "restricted," meaning "no Jews," American Jews are gen-

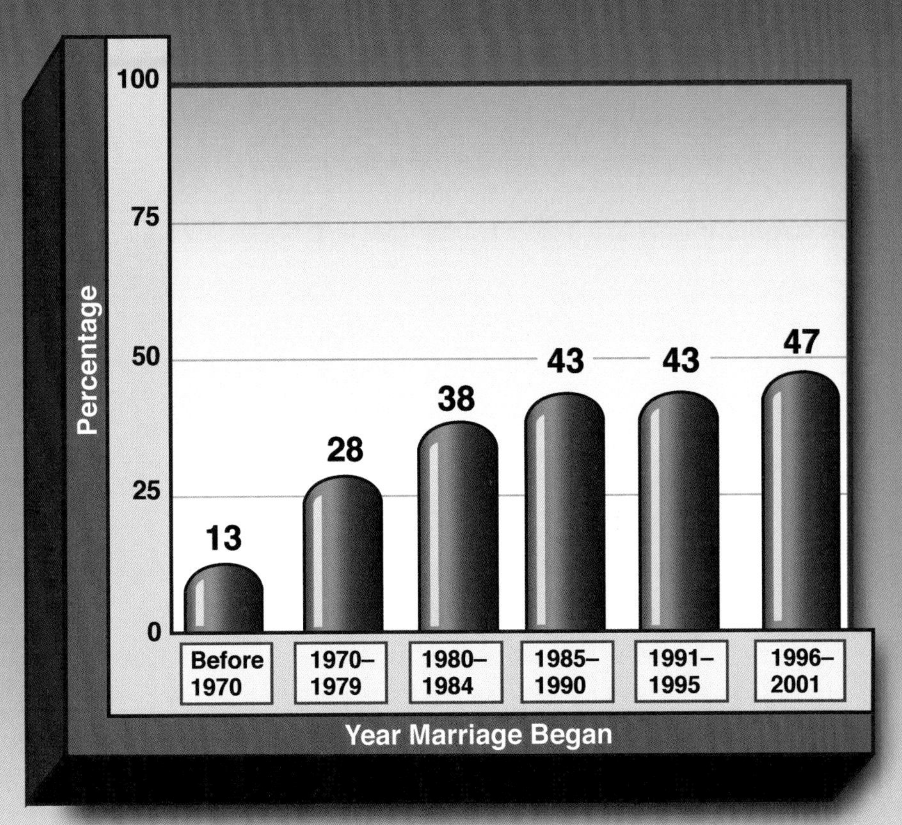

Taken from: United Jewish Communities National Jewish Population Survey, "Rates of Intermarriage," 2001.

erally free to live where they wish. Jewish "quotas," common until after World War II, are almost non-existent today, so Jews may freely attend the schools and universities of our choice. And (partly because it's the law) Jews may work wherever they want. What better places than the neighborhood, college and work place to meet a future spouse?

Secondly, Jews today are far more willing to marry a non-Jew than they were even one generation ago. Jews choose to marry non-Jews (just as non-Jews choose to marry Jews) for reasons of love and commitment; because of the conviction that "this is the person with whom I wish to share my life." Intermarrying Jews are also not per se rejecting either their heritage or their Jewishness. One need only read *The New York Times* on any Sunday, note the very high proportion of obvious intermarriages at which a rabbi or cantor officiates, to realize that

Edmund Case, left, and Rabbi Lev Baesh started a free referral service for interfaith couples who want a rabbi to officiate at their weddings.

in so many cases intermarriage neither involves rejection nor denial of the Jewish heritage.

Finally, non-Jewish Americans have generally accepted Jews and are no longer shocked by interfaith dating and intermarried couples. National public opinion surveys suggest that the acceptance of Jews as marriage partners among the broad cross-section of America has increased from about forty-five percent in the early 1960s to nearly eighty percent by the end of the 1980s. Even if the average American non-Jewish family would prefer that their son or daughter not marry a Jew, the freedom described above has exposed them to Jews in the community, the school, and the place of employment to a far greater degree than experienced by their own mothers and fathers.

Choosing Judaism

The creation, and success of the State of Israel not to mention the selection of Senator Joseph Lieberman as the first Jewish candidate for Vice President of the Democratic Party, has also helped to change many views about the "Jewish stereotype." Likewise, the civil rights movement in the United States, in which Jews had been so visibly active through the 1960s, has further helped to change perceptions about group boundaries. As a matter of fact, the social boundaries have become so porous that Jews-by-birth can drift away from their ancestral heritage as easily as non-Jews can drift into the community through intermarriage.

In our open society, every Jew is, in a fundamental sense, a "Jew by choice." That reality has led many of us to the recognition that the Jewishness of each family needs to be nurtured and enhanced—regardless of whether the partners are both born as Jews or whether the family includes an intermarried Jew and a non-Jewish spouse. We must not write them off, nor should we abandon their children to the natural assimilatory forces of the great American melting pot. They are all Jewish to some degree. Our task ought to be increasing the percentage of those who choose to become Jews fully or, at least, infusing more Jewishness into their lives.

EVALUATING THE AUTHORS' ARGUMENTS:

The author of the viewpoint you just read, David G. Sacks, believes that intermarriage is evidence of the strength and endurance of the Jewish community. The author of the previous viewpoint, Alexa Witt, disagrees. She argues that intermarriage weakens the Jewish people as a whole. Review both arguments, then state with which one you agree. Explain your reasoning.

Meaningful Judaism Can Exist Without God

"Humanistic Judaism seeks to integrate the value of Jewish identity with a belief in the value of human reason and human power."

Marti Keller

Marti Keller is a Unitarian minister in Atlanta. In the following viewpoint Keller states that she finds meaning in Judaism and identifies with her Jewish heritage despite the absence of God in her religious life. "Secular" or Humanistic Judaism focuses on compassion, kindness, and self-examination, Keller writes, and is accepting even of someone like her, an ordained Unitarian minister. The issue of God's existence, Keller states, is not important in her quest for a meaningful religious life.

AS YOU READ, CONSIDER THE FOLLOWING QUESTIONS:

1. Describe the main tenet of the Ethical Cultural Society.
2. In what year and by whom was Humanistic Judaism founded?
3. How does a traditional Jew, as opposed to a Humanistic Jew, define who is a Jew?

Marti Keller, "Growing Up a (Unitarian) Humanist Jew: Reason and Celebration," *Revmartikeller.com*, September 17, 2006. Reproduced by permission.

Growing up in a zealously secular Jewish home meant [attending a Unitarian Sunday school], and it meant Christmas trees with elk antlers for a star, meant no bibles or religious literature of any kind but books like [British philosopher] Bertrand Russell's *Why I Am Not a Christian.* It meant never going inside a synagogue, except for my Uncle Irving's wedding, never attending a Passover Seder, but once in a while watching my dad eating borscht and sour cream, or talking about some of the other foods he loved as a child in an ironically Kosher home. Or occasionally (and for me wonderfully) slipping in some Yiddish, telling us about the beloved characters of Yiddish culture.

My exposure to explicit Jewishness was almost the same, I can only imagine, as exposure to secular culture is for the children of fundamentalists. I remember reading the *Diary of Anne Frank* [a young Holocaust victim], almost secretively, learning through her about the Holocaust for example.

After carting us to one Unitarian congregation (or church) or another as younger children, as soon as we could get ourselves to youth group in other ways, my father became an entirely lapsed UU [Unitarian Universalist] and found an Ethical Culture Society, a place I imagine we all might have landed if there had been one available. Ethical Culture, founded by Felix Adler, was founded by a Jew with the intention of severing his particular ties to Judaism and even Jewish identity for what is described as "a religion of humanity, committed to the supreme value that all humans, whatever their race, religion, gender or political persuasion, are to be treated fairly and compassionately as fellow humans in one human family."

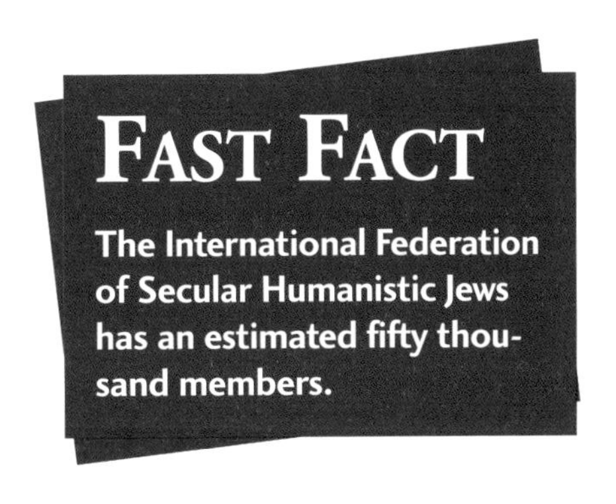

A Secular Alternative to Judaism

Within Ethical Culture, I imagine that my father found the resonances of the best of what I see as Jewish values, the inherently humanistic nature of essential Judaism, that as its "credo statement" puts it, Ethical Culture affirms that the supreme end of human life is to live in such a way that we acknowledge the worth, dignity and uniqueness of every human being (what theistic Jews describe as being created in the image of God) and work towards both personal relationships and broader social reform to encourage and enable all to develop their full human capacities.

Whether originally so or not, contemporary Ethical Culture identifies as being a religious community, based on current understandings of various religions around the world, many of which do not require belief in a supernatural being or supernatural reality. Ethical Culturists cite new definitions of religious affection, including one by Arthur Dobrin, a professor at Hofstra University, which states that religion is that set of beliefs and/or institutions, behaviors and emotions that binds human beings to something beyond their individual selves and fosters in its adherents a sense of humility and gratitude, that in turn sets the tone of one's world-view. In other words, he has written, religion connects a person to the larger world and creates a loyalty that extends to the past, present, and the future.

This philosophical community, this religion, was sufficient for my father for many years, as he assumed leadership positions including Presidency of the Palo Alto California society. Eventually, literally the call of the wild was stronger than his ties, even to this, as he increasingly took off every weekend for nature spots where he could watch and count birds.

Finding a Place as a Jew

Typical, very typical of third generation Jews, and also because I married a minimally religious Jew (and then another), this break off from Judaism without any ritual connections, with no holidays or holy days, was not ultimately appealing. When I became a mother, I found no conflict at all between remaining faithfully connected to the Berkeley Unitarian Church, teaching in the religious education program, attending services, while beginning to drop in on community High Holy Day services—the most liberal I could find—and finding friends who invited us to Seders while I learned what they were and eventually made our own. The God talk was never comfortable [for] me, but I could relate on an amazingly deep level to the metaphors of struggle and exile and liberation. The universalism within these stories and rituals, and the particular history of the Jewish people.

Liberal movements in Israel have been trying to attract secular Jews using advertisements like this billboard in Jerusalem stating, "There is more than one way to be a Jew."

Why did I not affiliate with Humanistic Judaism then, a nontheistic alternative in Jewish life that in many ways combines the moral/philosophical underpinnings of Ethical Culture with some of the rituals and ceremonies of more traditional Judaism, without God?

Very simply it did not exist as I grew up, in fact only was founded in 1963 by Rabbi Sherwin Wine in his previously Reform temple in Birmingham, Michigan. Humanistic Judaism describes itself as a human-centered philosophy that combines rational thinking with a celebration of Jewish culture that offers a genuine expression of their contemporary view of life. Humanistic Jewish communities celebrate Jewish holidays and life cycle events (such as weddings and bar and bat mitsva) with ceremonies that draw upon but go beyond traditional literature.

Traditional vs. Humanistic Judaism

In comparing itself to traditional affirmations of Judaism, what it means to be a Jew:

- Traditionally, a Jew is someone born of a Jewish mother, while in Humanistic Judaism a Jew is someone who identifies with the history, culture, struggles, triumphs and future of the Jewish people.
- Both traditional Jews and Humanistic Jews believe the preservation of Jewish identity, the survival of the remaining Jewish people, is important.
- Traditional Jews believe that Judaism is the religion of the Jewish people.
- Humanistic Jews believe that Judaism is the historic culture of the Jewish people.
- Traditional Jews believe that Jewish history is the saga of the relationship between God and a chosen people.
- Humanistic Jews believe that Jewish history is a saga of human behavior.
- Traditional Jews believe we are God's creatures and must live according to his commandments.
- Humanistic Jews believe we have the power and responsibility to shape our own lives independent of supernatural authority.
- Traditional Jews believe that ethics and morality flow from obedience to God and the laws of the Torah.
- Humanistic Jews believe that ethics and morality should serve human needs.
- Traditional Jews believe that the goal of Jewish morality is to fulfill our obligations to God and humanity as expressed in Halakha [Jewish law].
- Humanistic Jews believe that the goal of Jewish morality is the preservation of human dignity and integrity for ourselves and others.
- Ultimately, Humanistic Judaism seeks to integrate the value of Jewish identity with a belief in the value of human reason and human power.
- Humanistic Judaism declares itself free from supernatural authority. Humanistic philosophy affirms that knowledge and power come from

people and that the solutions to human problems can be found in the natural world.

- Humanistic Judaism seeks to promote the dignity of all people. Life is worthwhile when people see themselves as worthwhile.
- Humanistic Judaism holds that Judaism is the creation of the Jewish people. It is the celebration of the Jewish experience. Humanistic Judaism has its roots in this experience, in the history and culture of the Jewish people.
- Jewish holidays are responses to human events. Life cycle ceremonies are celebrations of human development. Music and literature are the expression of human needs.

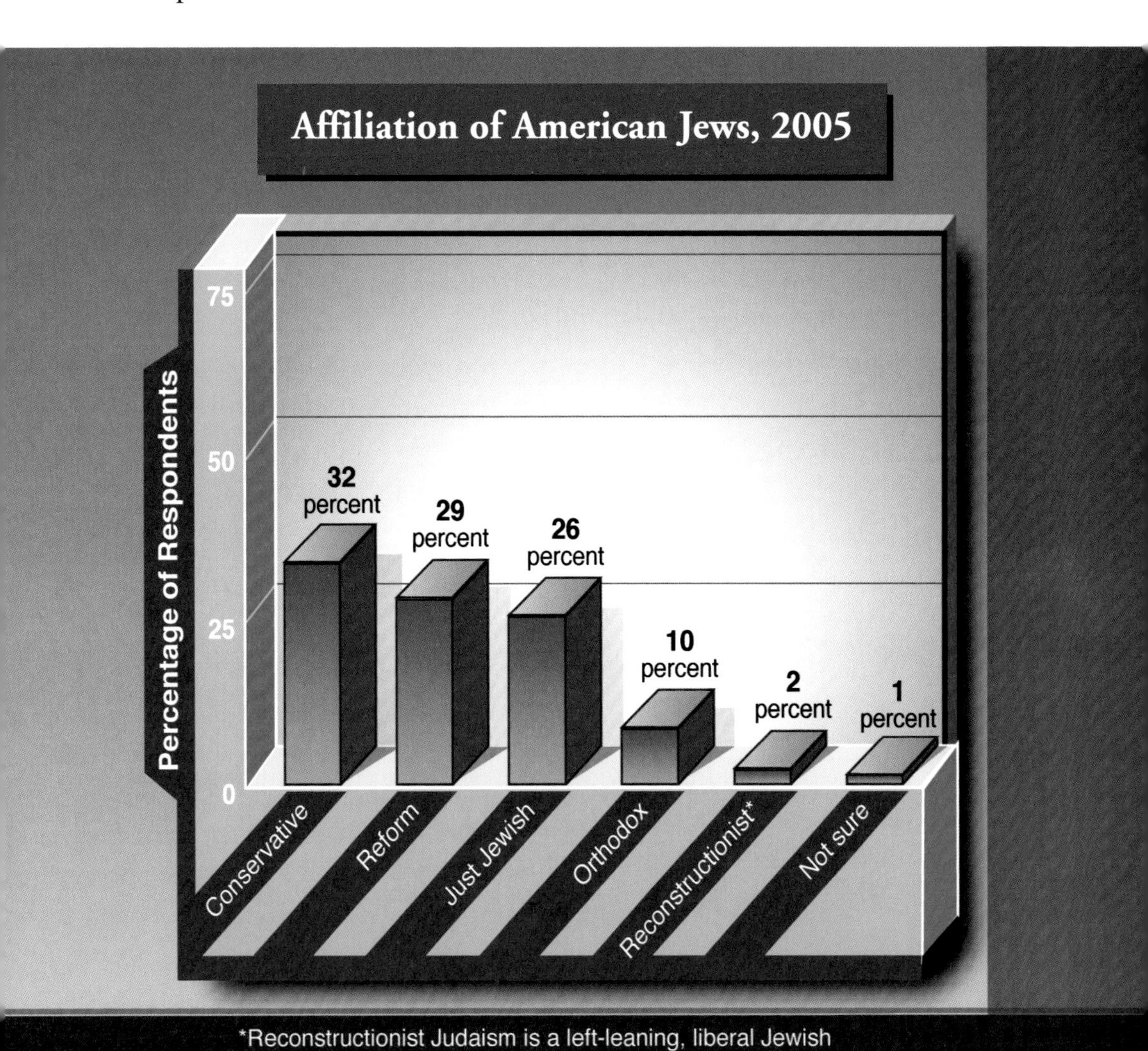

Taken from: American Jewish Committee, "2005 Annual Survey of American Jewish Opinion," 2005.

- Humanistic Jews want to educate themselves about historical Judaism and Jewish history, to understand the beliefs and behaviors of their ancestors without feeling compelled to agree with the beliefs of the past. They want their children to develop their own convictions honestly, on the basis of knowledge, not indoctrination.
- Humanistic Jews endorse ideals derived from the Jewish experience—democracy, justice, tolerance, pluralism and the equal treatment for all individuals.

Balancing Two Religious Communities

These premises, this combination of secular and cultural identity, this rich mix of reason and celebration, is what appeals to me in Humanistic Judaism. I cannot say that I might not have become exclusively a Humanistic Jew had this tiny denomination been available to me as a youth and a younger adult. At this point, I have spent more than 50 years as a Unitarian, an actively involved lay person and for the past almost decade as an ordained member of its clergy. There is too much about our religious community and movement in my blood and soul to abandon it completely.

I am in the process, however, of a dual professional affiliation, seeking to be recognized, if not as a Humanistic Rabbi (how cool it would be to be a Rabbi-Reverend, probably the first ever) but what is called a Madrikh, meaning guide, assuming pararabbinic leadership in Humanistic Judaism. I have become involved in revitalizing the small Humanistic Jewish havurah [fellowship] here in Atlanta, formerly called Kol Chaim (or community of life), and was [in 2005] invited as a speaker for the bi-annual convention of Humanistic Judaism.

Not reading or speaking a word of actual Hebrew, never having attended a Jewish service or Sunday school as a child, this feels to me like an almost overwhelming challenge. But this is the Jewish life I would like to live, the Jewish identity I want to have, the Jewish soul I wish to claim.

The question for me about God, like the question about God for Humanistic Jews, is what has been described as ignosticism (the question of God's existence is not primary). I chose to focus on things, as it has been said, that I can determine and affect, such as my relationships with other people, and improving the world around me.

Which in Hebrew is called Tikkun Olam—restoring and repairing a troubled world.

EVALUATING THE AUTHOR'S ARGUMENTS:

In the viewpoint you just read, author Marti Keller states that she believes it is possible to live a meaningful religious life without considering God's existence primary. She also states that she has spent fifty years as a Unitarian Universalist, yet she identifies with Humanistic Judaism. Do you think that her affiliation with another religious community gives her argument more credence, less, or makes no difference? Why?

Jewish Boys Should Not Necessarily Be Circumcised

"When you take the religion out of circumcision, and really look at what the procedure . . . involves, it is easy to see why more and more people are choosing to leave their sons intact."

Stacey Greenberg

Stacey Greenberg is a writer and editor in Memphis, Tennessee. In the following viewpoint Greenberg offers a personal vignette defending her decision not to circumcise her newborn son, even though she is Jewish. Greenberg writes that because of the modern information to which she had access via the Internet, she was able to make an informed decision, even though it differed from Jewish tradition. Greenberg writes that her desire to raise her son in a natural way included keeping all of the body parts with which he was born, including his foreskin.

AS YOU READ, CONSIDER THE FOLLOWING QUESTIONS:

1. What is one thing circumcision symbolizes, according to the author?
2. What does the author credit the Internet with allowing her to have?
3. Name two things the reform movement does in their effort to treat the sexes equally.

In the land before children, my husband and I had many a circumcision debate over dinner and drinks with friends. I always humored him as he made the comparison between circumcision and female genital mutilation, secretly knowing that I would trump his concerns with my Judaism card. He had agreed to a Jewish wedding and a Jewish household, and well, Jews circumcised their boys. End of story.

I'm not the most religious Jew ever, and my friends and husband have often wondered how I can even call myself a Jew. (Obviously they are not Jewish!) I can only say that being Jewish is just something I am, whether I attend synagogue on a regular basis or remember Shabbat or eat BBQ or whatever. I am a Jew. And there are certain things that even a reform Jew holds dear and circumcision is one of them. It symbolizes our covenant with G-d. It is what has identified us, at least those of us with penises, throughout the centuries. Circumcision is not something that a "good" Jew questions. It is a given.

Circumcision Is a Difficult Decision

Once I actually became pregnant, I assumed I was having a girl. I, like many Jewish mothers before me, wanted a girl in part because I didn't want to deal with the circumcision issue. Debating it over drinks and actually doing it are two completely different things. As my belly grew, so did my suspicion that I was having a boy. (Of course we could have found out for sure, but again I humored my husband's wish not to know until the birth.)

Around 30 weeks into my pregnancy, I decided I better deal with the circumcision issue. All discussions with my husband ended in a stalemate. I decided to schedule a meeting with a rabbi so we could gang up on him.

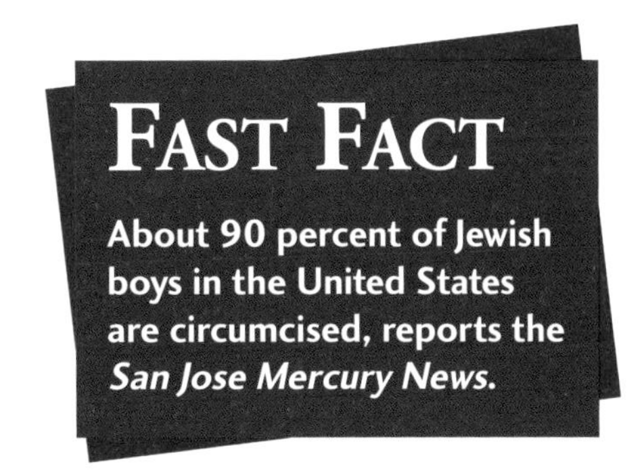

The rabbi who married us had since retired, so I had my choice of three other rabbis: A forty-ish up-and-comer with three girls in their tweens, a female in her thirties with a one-year-old son, and a new guy I didn't know much about. I went with the female, Rabbi Cohen. I figured she could speak from personal experience and that the issues would be fresh in her mind.

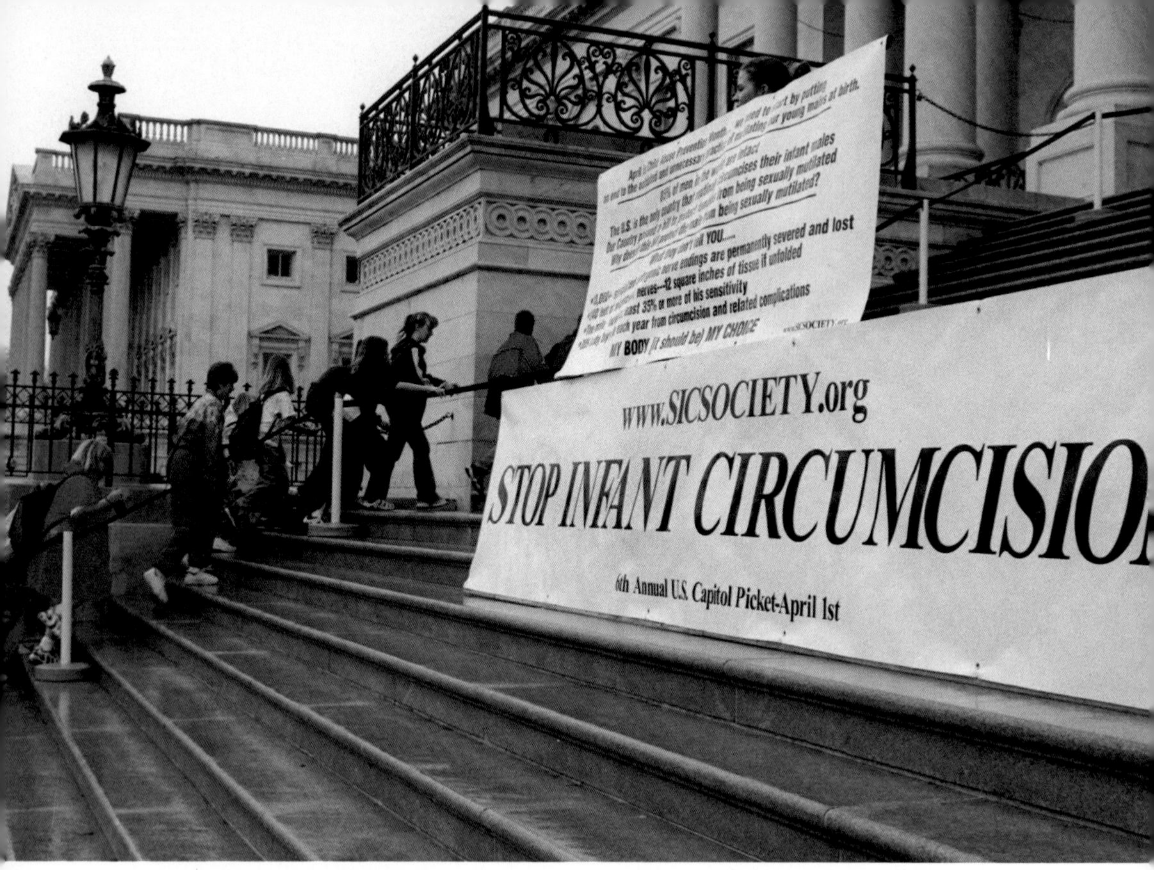

Circumcision, an accepted tradition for many years, has become a controversial decision for many.

Between the time I made the appointment with the rabbi and the time we were actually scheduled to go, I got an email from my friend who is a practicing midwife in California begging me to reconsider my decision. I don't know if she witnessed a recent circumcision or what, but she was adamant. I went through the Jewish rigmarole with her and she responded with a link to [anti-circumcision Web site] Nocirc.org and specifically said to look at the information on Judaism and circumcision.

What I found shocked me. There were stories of Jews from all over the United States who had decided not to circumcise their children. Not only were they talking about it, they were making it seem ok. And most importantly, they were still accepted in the Jewish community. I couldn't believe it. For the first time, I let myself really consider not circumcising my son. I also let myself read the circumcision boards at Mothering.com (which are decidedly anti-circumcision). I even found a few Jewish moms there who had kept their sons intact. I did a lot of soul searching and a lot of typing.

Examining the Procedure

When you take the religion out of circumcision, and really look at what the procedure actually involves, it is easy to see why more and more people are choosing to leave their sons intact. I thank my lucky stars for the Internet and the information it provided me on circumcision (as well as a million other mommy related questions). The Internet has allowed me to question the status quo; to find out why things are they way they are. A privilege our foremothers did not have. For me, the mere thought of giving birth to my precious baby at home without any medical intervention and then cutting off a part of his body eight days later just seemed absurd. I told myself that if G-d created my son with a foreskin, then he was going to keep it.

My husband was both thrilled and annoyed by my change of heart. Thrilled that I had "seen the light," but annoyed that it wasn't due to anything he had said. He was placated by the fact that I was now much more in agreement with him on the non-religious reasons to leave a child intact. However, I still felt like we should talk to the rabbi and ask that she perform a naming ceremony, not a bris, on the eighth day of our child's life, even if it was a boy.

In the reform tradition, there is a concerted effort to treat the sexes equally. At Temple Israel our prayer books are gender neutral and the prominent women in the Old Testament are mentioned just as often as the men. In the spirit of equality, reform rabbis started doing naming ceremonies for girls to welcome them into the Jewish community in the same way that a boy is welcomed into the community after he has a bris, or circumcision. I have to say that I am glad that in the quest for equality they decided circumcising girls was not the answer, but I believe that all boys and girls should remain intact upon entering the Jewish community.

An Alternative Ceremony

Our meeting with Rabbi Cohen definitely did not go as I had expected. For some reason, armed with my newfound information, I expected her to immediately admit that circumcision was barbaric and not necessary for all Jewish boys. Instead, she told us how beautiful her son's bris was, and how quickly and easily he healed. Undeterred, I

More Men and Boys Are Uncircumcised than in the Past

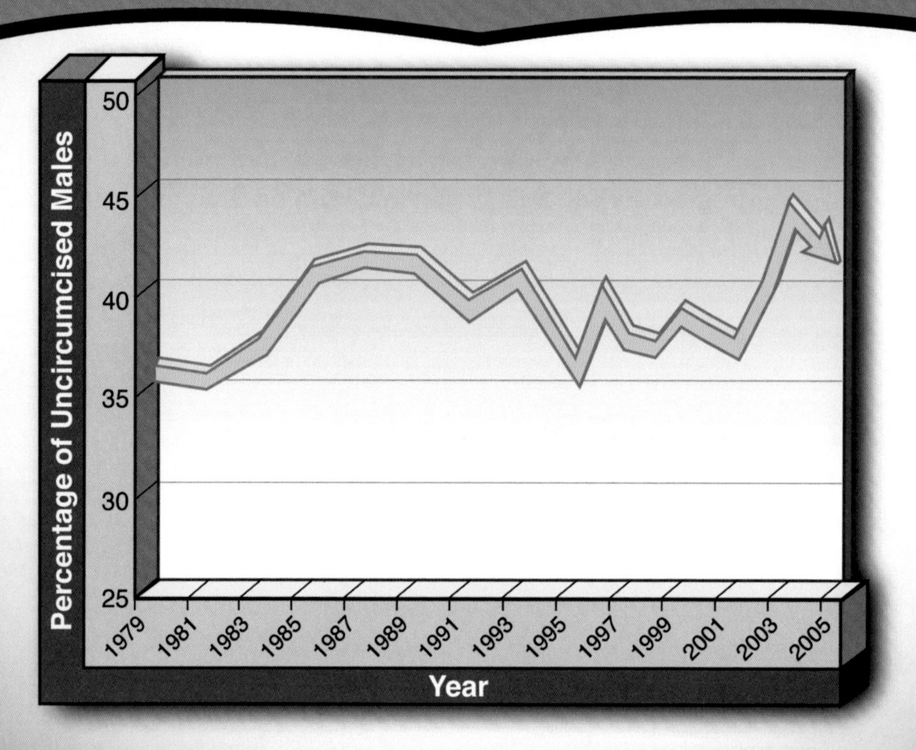

Taken from: The Circumcision Reference Library, "United States Circumcision Incidence," March 2, 2006.

shared with her the information I had downloaded from the Internet. I also told her of our plans to have a homebirth and our desire to raise our children as "naturally" as possible. I'm pretty sure she thought we were hippie freaks, but she played along. It all came down to one sticking point: The Jewish law that states that a child born of a Jewish mother is Jewish no matter what. (The law does not rely on circumcision to establish a Jewish identity because there is a caveat that states if a Jew loses a child due to complications from circumcision, future children are not required to be circumcised.) Rabbi Cohen thumbed through a few books, did an Internet search or two, and finally said, "Ok. I'll do a naming ceremony, no problem." It really was that easy. However, when I offered to speak to anyone else she might come across with similar desires, she made it clear that this wasn't something she planned to advertise or encourage.

On April 21, 2002, I gave birth to a healthy boy at home. Eight days later we rounded up every Jew we knew and had Rabbi Cohen perform a naming ceremony. We chose Shlomo Nitzan ("Peace Bud") as our son's Hebrew name and by the end of the ceremony there wasn't a dry eye in the room. Rabbi Cohen told our friends and family that she felt that Warren and I would be great parents because we cared enough about our child to research difficult issues and carefully consider everything before deciding what was best for our family. I couldn't have asked for more.

EVALUATING THE AUTHOR'S ARGUMENTS:

The author of the viewpoint you just read, Stacey Greenberg, is the mother of a Jewish boy. She always assumed she would have her son circumcised as is tradition in the Jewish faith, but when faced with the reality of the situation, she changed her mind. Where did she find support for her decision and where did she meet resistance? Do you believe it is appropriate for people to reconsider religious traditions based on new information?

Facts About Judaism

Editor's note: These facts can be used in reports or papers to reinforce or add credibility when making important points or claims.

Judaism in the United States

- Most American Jews belong to one of three major denominations of Judaism: Orthodox, Conservative, or Reform. Orthodox Jews can be further subdivided into ultra-Orthodox and modern Orthodox.
- The National Jewish Population Survey of 2000–2001, the last comprehensive study of American Jewry, estimates the number of Jews in the United States at 5.2 million, down from 5.5 million in 1990.
- According to the Baylor Institute for Studies of Religion, only 2.5 percent of the American population identify themselves as Jewish. By comparison, 60 percent are Protestant, 21 percent identify as Catholic, and 11 percent of those surveyed say they are unaffiliated with any religion.

Judaism and Tradition

- Jewish law calls for boys to be circumcised eight days after their birth in a ceremony called *brit milah*, which translates as "the covenant of circumcision."
- Jews refer to the first five books of the Old Testament as the Torah and consider it their holy text. Observant Jews also follow extensive sets of rules written in a medieval book called the Talmud.
- Some Jews follow a set of dietary restrictions called kosher laws. Some of the restrictions include: not eating pork and shellfish, not eating meat and dairy together, and slaughtering food animals in a specific manner.

Judaism Through History

- Judaism is the world's oldest monotheistic religion. Jews date the beginning of their religion from 1800 B.C. when Jewish tradition holds that the Biblical patriarch Abraham made a covenant, or sacred agreement, with God.

- The first Jewish people arrived in what would become the United States in 1654, settling in New Amsterdam, now New York, according to the American Jewish Committee.
- In 1909 Jewish and African American leaders worked together to create the National Association for the Advancement of Colored People (NAACP). Many Jews joined African Americans in sit-ins and freedom rides during the civil rights movement of the 1960s.
- According to the public television movie *From Swastika to Jim Crow*, 50 percent of civil rights attorneys in the South during the 1960s were Jewish.

The Holocaust

- During World War II the Nazis referred to their plan to kill all the Jews of Europe as the "Final Solution." By the time the war was over, 6 million Jews had been killed, representing two-thirds of the European Jewish population, according to the Jewish Virtual Library.
- Almost all of the Jews in Poland were killed during the Holocaust. According to the Shoah Resource Center at Yad Vashem, Israel's Holocaust museum, as many as 3 million of Poland's 3.3 million Jews were exterminated.

According to a January 2007 survey by the British Holocaust Memorial Day Trust:

- 41 percent of Britons surveyed believe another Holocaust is possible.
- 36 percent believe most people would stand by and do nothing were genocide to erupt in the UK.
- 50 percent of those surveyed are unaware that lesbians, gays, and the disabled were also persecuted by the Nazis, in addition to Jews.

Anti-Semitism

According to the Anti-Defamation League's 2007 Survey of American Attitudes Towards Jews in America:

- Approximately 15 percent or 35 million Americans hold anti-Semitic views, up from 14 percent in 2005.
- Anti-Semitic views tend to decrease as the level of a person's education increases. For instance, 21 percent of those surveyed who have a high school degree or less hold anti-Semitic views, while only 8 percent of those with post-graduate degrees do.
- More men than women hold anti-Semitic views, particularly men who are unmarried and do not have a college degree.

Glossary

anti-Semitism: Discrimination against or hostility toward Jews or Judaism.

circumcision: The surgical removal of the foreskin, the skin that covers the tip of the penis, usually performed soon after birth. Circumcision is a religious ceremony among Jews and Muslims.

genocide: The deliberate and planned extermination of a national, racial, political, or cultural group.

Gentile: A person who is not Jewish. The term is often used by Jews to refer to non-Jews.

intermarriage: Marriage between a man and woman from different races, religions, social classes, or ethnic groups.

Jewry: A collective term for the Jewish people.

Judeo-Christian: Relating to the traditions, rituals, or values of the Jewish and Christian people. The term refers to the shared religious origins of the two groups.

nationalism: The assertion of the interests of one's own nation, as separate from the interests of other nations or the common interests of all nations.

Unitarian: A liberal Christian religious group that believes that God is universal, all humans receive salvation, and reason and conscience should be the basis for belief and practice.

vilify: To slander or make vicious or cruel statements about.

Zionism: The movement to protect and promote the interests of the state of Israel. Zionism first arose in the late nineteenth century in response to growing anti-Semitism and advocated for the establishment of a Jewish state in what was then Palestine.

Organizations to Contact

The editors have compiled the following list of organizations concerned with the issues debated in this book. The descriptions are derived from materials provided by the organizations. All have publications or information available for interested readers. The list was compiled on the date of publication of the present volume; the information provided here may change. Be aware that many organizations take several weeks or longer to respond to inquiries, so allow as much time as possible.

Aish International
1 Western Wall Plaza, PO Box 14149
Jerusalem, Israel 91141
(972-2) 628-5666
fax: (972-2) 627-3172
e-mail: info@aish.com
Web site: www.aish.com

Aish International is a conservative religious organization that operates learning centers in various locations throughout the world, including Jerusalem. Aish runs educational and religious programs aimed at fostering traditional Jewish values and beliefs. The organization maintains extensive online resources at its Web site, including articles on topics relevant to Jewish life.

American Jewish Committee (AJC)
PO Box 705
New York, NY 10150
(212) 751-4000
fax: (212) 891-1450
e-mail: newyork@ajc.org
Web site: www.ajc.org

The AJC is an international think tank and advocacy organization that supports Israel's efforts for peace and security, strengthening American Jewish ties to Israel, and combating bigotry and anti-Semitism. The organization runs public awareness and education campaigns and community events to bring about its goals. The AJC publishes *The American Jewish Year Book* annually as well as articles on subjects including Jewish life, the Holocaust, and Israel on its Web site.

American Jewish World Service (AJWS)
45 West Thirty-sixth St.
New York, NY 10018
(212) 792-2900
fax: (212) 792-2930
e-mail: ajws@ajws.org
Web site: www.ajws.org

The AJWS is an international development organization that functions on Judaism's principle of justice. Through volunteer efforts, grassroots advocacy, and public awareness campaigns, the organization seeks to end hunger and poverty among all the world's people. The AJWS publishes regular bulletins on its errors, as well as op-ed pieces and viewpoints in major newspaper and magazines.

Anti-Defamation League (ADL)
PO Box 96226
Washington, DC 20090
(202) 452-8310
fax: (202) 296-2371
e-mail: washington-dc@adl.org
Web site: www.adl.org

The ADL is a nonprofit advocacy group that seeks to end discrimination against Jews and all people through the collection and dissemination of information about anti-Semitism, bigotry, and prejudice. The ADL publishes an annual report detailing its findings, as well as *Connections*, a monthly newsletter; the *International Report*; and *On Guard*, a security report.

B'nai B'rith International
2020 K St. NW
Washington, DC 20006
(202) 857-6600

e-mail: website@bnaibrith.org
Web site: www.bnaibrith.org

B'nai B'rith is a youth-based international humanitarian and social action organization dedicated to increasing Jewish identity awareness and supporting Israel. B'nai B'rith runs summer camps and youth leadership programs throughout the country, as well as volunteer programs. The group publishes many newsletters and brochures, including the magazine *B'nai B'rith*, and *Dor L'Dor*, a giving-focused newsletter.

Jewish Circumcision Resource Center (JCRC)
PO Box 232
Boston, MA 02133
(617) 523-0088
e-mail: jcrc@jewishcircumcision.org
Web site: www.jewishcircumcision.org

This division of the Circumcision Resource Center aims to protest the tradition of religious circumcision of Jewish boys. The JCRC works to provide nontraditional Jewish parents with information and support in their decision not to circumcise. The center has published the book *Questioning Circumcision: A Jewish Perspective.*

Jewish Women's Archive (JWA)
38 Harvard St.
Brookline, MA 02446
(617) 232-2258
fax: (617) 975-0109
Web site: www.jwa.org

The JWA is a nonprofit group dedicated to recording and preserving Jewish women's history globally, nationally, and locally. The JWA maintains its archive of documents on its Web site and provides lesson plans so that teachers may use the archive for teaching purposes. In addition to the archival documents, the group maintains a blog, Jewesses with Attitude.

Meretz USA
114 West Twenty-sixth St., Suite 1002
New York, NY 10001

(212) 242-4500
fax: (212) 242-5718
e-mail: mail@meretzusa.org
Web site: www.meretzusa.org

Meretz USA is a liberal nonprofit organization that supports peace between Israel and its neighbors, including the Palestinians. The organization seeks to draw awareness to the issue of conflict in the Middle East through rallies, public awareness campaigns, and lectures. Meretz USA publishes a blog by the same name, as well as the quarterly magazine *Israel Horizons.*

United Jewish Communities (UJC)
PO Box 30, Old Chelsea Station
New York, NY 10113
(212) 284-6500
e-mail: info@ujc.org
Web site: www.ujc.org

The UJC is the umbrella organization for the Jewish Federations, groups that provide humanitarian assistance to Jews in need throughout the world, with a special focus on Israel. The UJC and the federations solicit funds in order to support these operations, as well as encourage general philanthropy among American Jews. The UJC maintains extensive resources on its Web site and publishes an annual report.

Wexner Foundation
8000 Walton Pkwy., Suite 110
New Albany, OH 43054
(614) 930-6060
e-mail: info@wexner.net
Web site: www.wexnerheritage.org

The Wexner Foundation is a privately funded, nonprofit organization that focuses on training Jewish professional and volunteer leaders, as well as supporting public leaders in Israel. The foundation offers an array of scholarships and fellowships and runs a heritage program. The organization publishes the weekly newsletter *Jewish Leadership Resources.*

World Jewish Congress (WJC)
PO Box 90400
Washington, DC 20090

(212) 755-5770
e-mail: info@worldjewishcongress.org
Web site: www.worldjewishcongress.org

The WJC is an international nongovernmental organization that works to promote the needs of Jews around the world. The congress has a diplomatic seat at the United Nations where it works to ensure that its goal of security and peace for Jewish communities is met. The WJC also runs a research institute and publishes the scholarly *Israel Journal of Foreign Affairs.*

Zionist Organization of America (ZOA)
4 East Thirty-fourth St.
New York, NY 10016
(212) 481-1500
fax: (212) 481-1515
e-mail: info@zoa.org
Web site: www.zoa.org

The ZOA is a conservative, right-wing lobbying group that seeks to promote support of Israel in the media, on college campuses, and in Congress. The group runs a Campus Activism Network aimed at mobilizing pro-Israel college students and operates a legal center, the Center for Law and Justice, which takes on Israel-based legal issues. The ZOA publishes an annual report and runs regular ads in newspapers and magazines supporting its positions.

For Further Reading

Books

Arthur Blecher, *The New American Judaism: The Way Forward on Challenging Issues from Intermarriage to Jewish Identity.* New York: Palgrave Macmillian, 2007. The author attempts to correct long-held misconceptions about traditional Judaism, claiming that American Jews have been misled about Jewish history and identity.

Noah Efron, *Real Jews: Secular Versus Ultra-Orthodox and the Struggle for Jewish Identity in Israel.* New York: Basic Books, 2003. A discussion of the issues confronting different groups of Jews in Israel and how those issues affect Jews as a whole.

Edward Feinstein, *Jews and Judaism in the 21st Century: Human Responsibility, the Presence of God and the Future of the Covenant.* Woodstock, VT: Jewish Lights, 2007. Discussions from five Jewish leaders on the duty of Jews in the twenty-first century and the state of modern Jewry.

Abraham H. Foxman, *The Deadliest Lies: The Israel Lobby and the Myth of Jewish Control.* New York: Palgrave Macmillian, 2007. An argument against the idea that there exists an Israel lobby that influences U.S. foreign policy decisions.

Saul Friedlander, *The Years of Extermination: Nazi Germany and the Jews 1939–1945.* New York: HarperCollins, 2007. This historical work recounts the collapse of Jewish life and culture in Europe as Nazi rule slowly grew stronger.

Jonathan C. Friedman, *Rainbow Jews: Jewish and Gay Identity in the Performing Arts.* Lanham, MD: Lexington Books, 2007. This book examines Jewish and gay culture in film and in the theater, covering the 1960s to present day.

Robert Goldenberg, *The Origins of Judaism: From Canaan to the Rise of Islam.* Cambridge, UK: Cambridge University Press, 2007. A history of ancient Judaism in Israel and the rest of the world from biblical times until the start of Islam.

Alfred Kolatch, *Inside Judaism: The Concepts, Customs and Celebrations of the Jewish People*. New York: Jonathan David, 2006. The author explores the relationship of Jewish thought to deeds and practice, covering a wide range of topics relevant to Jewish life.

Walter Laquer, *The Changing Face of Anti-Semitism: From Ancient Times to the Present Day*. Oxford, UK: Oxford University Press, 2006. A comprehensive history of anti-Semitism and its manifestations.

David Mamet, *The Wicked Son: Anti-Semitism, Self-Hatred, and the Jews*. New York: Schocken, 2006. A collection of essays analyzing the reasons behind anti-Semitism and self-prejudice both within the Jewish community and without.

Daniel Mendelsohn, *The Lost: A Search for Six of Six Million*. New York: HarperCollins. 2006. A memoir about the author's search for his family who died in the Holocaust.

Michael L. Morgan, *Interim Judaism: Jewish Thought in a Century of Crisis*. Bloomington: Indiana University Press, 2001. The author discusses a shift in Jewish values in the twentieth century and suggests that a new Judaism will emerge in the twenty-first.

Pamela Nadell, *American Jewish Women's History: A Reader*. New York: New York University Press, 2003. A collection of essays tracing the history and role of Jewish women in the United States from early twentieth century until present day.

George Robinson, *Essential Judaism: A Complete Guide to Beliefs, Customs and Rituals*. New York: Atria, 2001. An overview of Jewish theology, philosophy, and practice, including explanations of holidays, rituals, and laws.

Raymond P. Scheindlin, *A Short History of the Jewish People: From Legendary Times to Modern Statehood*. Oxford, UK: Oxford University Press, 2000. A history of Jewish communities around the world.

Alan E. Steinweis, *Studying the Jew: Scholarly Antisemitism in Nazi Germany*. Cambridge: Harvard University Press, 2006. An examination of the academic studies and reports that contributed to the "Final Solution" of the Holocaust.

Michael Strassfeld, *A Book of Life: Embracing Judaism as a Spiritual Practice*. Woodstock, VT: Jewish Lights, 2006. A guide to ethical

Jewish behavior and values and a discussion of Jewish spirituality, written by a rabbi.

Joseph Telushkin, *A Code of Jewish Ethics.* Vol 1: *You Shall Be Holy.* New York: Harmony/Bell Tower, 2006. An explanation of ethical Jewish behavior and instructions for how to live a sacred Jewish life.

Miryam Wahrman, *Brave New Judaism: When Science and Scripture Collide.* Boston: Brandeis University Press, 2004. This book attempts to apply Jewish precepts and law to modern medical situations, including stem cells, cloning, and genetic testing.

Ruth R. Wisse, *Jews and Power.* New York: Schocken, 2007. A survey of Jewish history, focusing on the Jewish political experience from biblical times to present.

Periodicals

Barbara Amiel, "A Plague Without a Cure," *Maclean's*, May 8, 2004.

Daphna Baram, "The Defeat of the Pork-Eaters," *New Statesman*, December 16, 2004.

Tsvi Blanchard, "Sharing Jerusalem," *Tikkun*, November/December 2006.

BR, "What America Believes," June 2004.

Economist, "Israel's Wasted Victory," May 26, 2006.

Mark Edmunson, "Defender of the Faith?" *New York Times Magazine*, September 9, 2007.

Barbara Ehrenreich, "All-American Anti-Semitism," *Progressive*, February 2007.

Don Feder, "Atheism Isn't the Final Word," *USA Today*, April 16, 2007.

Abraham H. Foxman, "Dialogue with Muslims: Reality or Pipe Dream?" *Jewish Week*, November 17, 2006.

———, "We Are One, but Not the Same," *Forward*, August 24, 2006.

David J. Goldberg, "Faith and Reason: There Is No Rise in Anti-Semitism Where I Live," *London Independent*, February 7, 2004.

Laurie Goodstein, "Conservative Jews Allow Gay Rabbis and Unions," *New York Times*, December 7, 2006.

Marjorie Ingall, "Why Are There So Many Jewish Feminists?" *Forward*, November 18, 2005.

Ronit Ir-Shai and Tamar Ross, "We're Not Against Motherhood," *Jerusalem Post*, May 21, 2006.

Efraim Karsh and Rory Miller, "Europe's Persecuted Muslims?" *Commentary*, April 2007.

William Kristol, "Anti-Judaism," *Wall Street Journal*, September 8, 2006.

Lucette Lagnado, "Prayer Behind the Partition," *Wall Street Journal*, May 23, 2007.

Daniel Lazare, "Among the Disbelievers," *Nation*, May 28, 2007.

Yitzhak Levanon, "Failure to Reject Anti-Semitism Risks Laying Groundwork for Future Murderous Regimes," *Jerusalem Post*, January 30, 2007.

Naday Morag, "Israel's Goals in the Present Conflict," *Christian Science Monitor*, July 20, 2006.

Mark Oppenheimer, "Join a Brownstone Shtetl," *New York*, January 22, 2007.

Yorke J. Peeler, "Lest We Forget. . ." *Christian Century*, May 20, 2007.

Michael Plitnick, "Who Speaks for Us?" *Tikkun*, July/August 2006.

Daniel Polish, "The Messiah Is Coming," *America*, September 24, 2007.

Stefan C. Reif, "With and Against the Jews," *TLS*, February 23, 2007.

Carlin Romano, "Who Took the 'Judeo' Out of 'Judeo-Christian?'" *Chronicle of Higher Education*, January 26, 2007.

Seymour Rossel, "Letting God In," *Cjcn.org*, June 1, 2007.

Noam Scheiber, "Black Hat Trick," *New Republic*, September 13, 2004.

William Schneider, "Aggressive Courtship," *National Journal*, May 28, 2004.

Michael A. Signer, "Seeing, Tasting, Telling," *America*, April 2, 2007.

Barbara Smith, "Back to Ethnic Cleansing?" *New Statesman*, July 12, 2004.

Craig S. Smith, "In Poland, a Jewish Revival Thrives—Minus Jews," *New York Times*, July 12, 2007.

Andrew Solomon, "The Loneliness of a Liberal U.S. Jew," *New Statesman*, October 25, 2004.

Toronto Star, "A 'Golden Age' of Intolerance," June 19, 2005.

Alan Wolfe, "Free Speech, Israel, and Jewish Illiberalism," *Chronicle of Higher Education*, November 17, 2006.

Web Sites

Conversion to Judaism Resource Center (www.convert.org). This Web site is the home page for the resource center. It offers articles and viewpoints on the conversion process as well as guides for those interested in converting to Judaism.

Jewish Virtual Library (www.jewishvirtuallibrary.org). This online archive contains many of the Judaic documents found in the Library of Congress on subjects that include history, biography, politics, women, Israel, and the Holocaust, among others.

Jews Against Circumcision (www.jewsagainstcircumcision.org). The group maintaining this Web site opposes circumcision, including those performed for both medical and religious reasons. The site includes a list of reasons not to circumcise, as well as a blog related to the issues.

Katrina's Jewish Voices (http://katrina.jwa.org). The Jewish Women's Archive collects stories of Jews affected by Hurricane Katrina in 2005 at this Web site. Visitors can contribute their own stories or read those of others, as well as browse photographs and other documents.

United States Holocaust Memorial Museum (www.ushmm.org). The official Web site for the Holocaust Memorial Museum in Washington, D.C., includes extensive Holocaust history, information, and online exhibits, including photographs.

Index

Picture Credits

Maury Aaseng, 15, 23, 28, 34, 38, 46, 52, 57, 63, 72, 78, 83, 91, 98
AP Images, 12, 17, 21, 29, 40, 48, 51, 59, 65, 74, 84, 89, 96
© Israel images/Alamy, 77
© David McNew/Getty Images, 70
© PeerPoint/Alamy, 44
© Pedro Ugarte/AFP/Getty Images, 33